Writing From Life

How to turn your personal experience into profitable prose

2ND EDITION

Lynne Hackles

howto

D1103447

Published by How To Books Ltd,
Spring Hill House, Spring Hill Road,
Begbroke, Oxford OX5 1RX. United Kingdom.
Tel: (01865) 375794. Fax: (01865) 379162.
info@howtobooks.co.uk
www.howtobooks.co.uk

How To Books greatly reduce the carbon footprint of their books by sourcing their
typesetting and printing in the UK.

British Library Cataloguing in Publication Data
A catalogue record for this book is available from the British Library

ISBN 978 1 84528 419 0

First published 2008
Second edition 2010

Produced for How To Books by Deer Park Productions, Tavistock, Devon
Typeset by PDQ Typesetting, Newcastle-under-Lyme, Staffs.
Printed and bound by Bell & Bain Ltd, Glasgow

NOTE: The material contained in this book is set out in good faith for general guidance
and no liability can be accepted for loss or expense incurred as a result of relying in
particular circumstances on statements made in the book. The laws and regulations are
complex and liable to change, and readers should check the current position with the
relevant authorities before making personal arrangements.

Contents

PART TWO — FICTION

1

Writing and Your Life

Where does writing come from? We are not talking Muse here. There should be no waiting for inspiration. So, without inspiration, where do the ideas for writing come from?

Research

You can research different subjects by visiting the library, surfing the Internet or talking to experts. Some writers love research. Some hate it. The good news is that you don't have to do any research if you don't want to.

Imagination

You can use your imagination. As a child you were probably told you had a *vivid imagination* and that's why you are a writer now. If you are scared of the dark you probably have too much imagination. (Can you have too much?)

Of course you need to use your imagination in order to write science fiction and fantasy but even then you'd need a final source in order for your readers to identify with your characters. You actually need imagination to write any sort of fiction but there are times when it can be difficult to drag ideas from your imagination. You need a starting point and this is where the final source of writing comes from.

PERSONAL EXPERIENCE

Many writers draw on their own experiences in order to write.
Every person they meet can become a character, every place they
visit is a possible setting, and every word they hear can be used as
dialogue in their stories and books. They dredge up memories,
good and bad. They explore their emotions. They rake over their
dramas and even manage to find a use for the trivial incidents
that happen in their lives.

It is how to turn a personal experience into a piece of work you
can sell that can cause the problem. This book will show you how.
It will also guide you through the endless opportunities to use
your personal experiences – everything from Readers' Letters to
articles, stories, poems, novels, how-to books. In fact almost
anything...

Personal experience used in any form of writing can make your
work stronger, more appealing and therefore give it more chance
of being published. Make good use of the emotions, traumas, joys
and experiences of your own life whether you are writing fiction or
non-fiction.

Recording a memory

All your personal experiences are in your memory banks but
memory is fickle. Don't count on remembering a sunset, cloud
formation, face or outfit, the way a passer-by walks, or a snatch of
dialogue. WRITE IT DOWN.

Memory is fleeting. Ideas and memories are like bubbles as they
pop to the surface of your consciousness but they soon turn into
pebbles and sink. Make notes whenever a memory bubbles up, so
that you don't forget it. You may think that you won't but, like

ideas, memories sink as quickly as they surface. You think the idea is so good, or the memory so glowing, that you will never forget it but if the flash of a remembered event comes while you're driving in traffic and then you have to concentrate on a blip in that traffic, the memory sinks like that heavy pebble, never to resurface. You wake in the night from a wonderful dream which reminds you of something from your childhood but you don't write it down and by morning it's forgotten. Of course, it may have been rubbish, but on the other hand ...

The good news is that memory has no boundaries. Our past becomes memories. Our present is happening now but in five minutes time that too will become our past and another memory for you to store. This means that we will have an endless supply of memories to draw on, and that will give us an endless supply of ideas to write about.

Your endless supply of ideas

How old are you? Did you answer 80? Or 55? 26? 14? Whatever your age you have that many years of personal experience to call upon. It's a daunting task and the longer the life, the more daunting the task or, looking on the positive side, the longer the life, the more material (personal experience) you have.

During the course of this book we will be building up a file listing your personal experiences. You will need a pen and a book to write in. This could be a cheap and plain exercise book or you might like to use an attractive hard-backed notebook. It's down to personal choice. Each time you open this book make sure your notebook and pen are to hand.

Exercises to help you recall personal experiences are given throughout these pages. Try them all and you will end up with a huge source of information to draw upon when you are writing. Later we'll be discovering how to put all this information to good use and how and where to get it published.

Let's start your Personal Experiences file now.

Where do I begin?

Let's start at the very beginning. You were born. You won't remember that but what is your earliest memory?

As my tester (husband) read that question he immediately said, 'I wore boxing gloves and my dressing gown and had my eye blacked. I was a boxer in the fancy dress procession on Coronation Day.'

When I was three I was a bridesmaid but do I really remember my Auntie hissing at me to hold up my posy of flowers or is this something I have been told? Perhaps I've made it up to fit the photograph I have of the occasion. Whichever way, it doesn't matter. If it is your personal experience or one that someone has bestowed upon you, then you can use it.

EXERCISE

Raking up your past. Write about your earliest memory. Don't stop to think. Begin with 'I remember' and carry on from there. Do it NOW.

USING MEMORY AIDS

So many years mean so many personal experiences and so much material to call upon. Do not despair. You have memory aids all around you and these will help dredge up all those wonderful, and not so wonderful, personal experiences. Some of these memory aids might include:

- photographs
- diaries
- personal possessions
- letters
- music
- family trees
- memory boxes.

As you search through these aids you will begin to realise that each picture, letter or item holds a story and that story is one of your personal experiences.

Looking at photographs

Spend an evening sorting through old albums and loose photographs. Keep your notebook by your side and as pictures remind you of personal experiences, write them down.

Try doing this in the company of a child or grandchild. They will ask all the questions – Who is that? Where are you? How old are you in that one? Did you like those funny clothes? Their questions will revive those memories.

Go and visit your parents, or grandparents and ask to browse the family albums. You could learn a lot.

My tester recalls a 50-year old photograph of himself with his grandfather. They are in the garden standing either side of a wheelbarrow. Last year an almost identical photograph was taken of him with his grandson, working alongside a wheelbarrow on our vegetable garden.

Reading diaries

Have you always wished you'd kept diaries? Have you several that have been carefully filled in for the first few weeks of January? Or do you have a collection stretching through the years back to childhood?

Diaries can be very useful. If you listed everyday events, part of your life will be recorded there. If you confessed your true feelings to your diary then you will have access to the way you felt at emotional times during your life.

Diaries can help with names, places and most importantly dates. They are records of your personal experiences.

Re-reading them may bring back all sorts of related events. For instance, while I was recording family holidays and jolly picnics in my school diary (heavily influenced by Enid Blyton), my parents were actually struggling to hold their marriage together. At that time I was oblivious to this. Now, as I read, the whole thing holds this sub-plot.

Thinking about personal possessions

Hoarders will have more to call upon. Most hoarders are reluctant to throw anything away because all of their possessions hold memories for them. They could tell you the history of each – where they had come from, how long they had owned them, who had bought them and why.

Do you have a treasured piece of furniture? Why does it mean so much to you? Write down the reasons.

A book holds an inscription to the best English student, or to my love... Other family heirlooms vibrate with their history. In fact, every item you own will hold a personal experience. Where did you buy it? Why did you buy it? Was it a gift? From whom? Try walking around your home and picking up items at random, then remembering as much about them as possible.

Don't forget to have your notebook with you so that you can write down the personal experiences relating to each item.

Re-reading letters

In the age of telephones and email are letters going to become extinct? Do you have any love-letters? Or letters from family living on the other side of the world? Do you have a bundle of letters that you haven't thought about for years, tucked away at the back of a drawer?

This is where hoarders have the advantage. If you don't throw belongings away then perhaps you are the owner of a letter collection. Read them through. What memories and emotions do they stir?

Listening to music

'They're playing our song?' Have you ever said that? Does any song have a special meaning for you? Why? If you were to play it now what personal experiences would it revive? Where were you when you first heard it? And who were you with?

The Beatles singing *Love Me Do* might whizz you back to the 1960s and an unrequited love. *Land of Hope and Glory* might stir war-time memories, or you may have listened to it when you were with a loved one at the Last Night of The Proms, or perhaps you have visited Elgar's birthplace.

What about the silly songs learned at school? Do you remember any and do they hold experiences for you? A child or grandchild singing the same songs might give your memory banks a nudge.

Examining family trees

If you, or a member of your family, is into genealogy then take a look at the family tree. You are who you are now because of those who went before you. As you read the names of relatives, alive and dead, some distant memories may surface. A great-grandfather giving you pocket money. An aged aunt teaching you how to knit. For this one, my tester remembered his grandfather telling him that as long as he had a ball of string, a penknife and a sixpence he could go around the world.

Keeping a memory box

A long time ago, before I realised that all your personal experiences and memories could be kept in your head, I used to save things. I kept a memory box. The first time I heard about these was in a letter to a women's magazine. The writer had described her box and how she kept mementoes in it. Thinking it was a good idea I decided to start my own. You could too. It's never too late.

Any box will do. It can be a cardboard shoe-box, a box-file or a beautiful box made from rare wood and inlaid with mother-of-pearl. If it is the latter then the box will be trembling with personal experiences of its own. Even the shoe-box will hold memories. My box originally belonged to my grandmother who passed it to my mother who kept her war-time love-letters inside it.

What sort of things do you put in your memory box? Memories, of course. Take a look at a few of mine.

- A ban the bomb badge.
- The box that held my wedding ring.
- The silver heart from our wedding cake.
- Hospital bracelets from when the children were born and from various hospital stays.
- The disc from my back, removed during one of those hospital stays. (It was given to me and I couldn't say no, and there was nowhere else to put it.)
- A decorated matchbox my son made for me when he was five.
- A letter my daughter sent me when she was six.
- Assorted invitations to weddings, parties, anniversaries, celebrations ...

You get the idea? Each item holds the memory of some personal experience from life – some several.

Perhaps one or more of the items in my memory box will start you thinking about something similar in your lives.

EXERCISE

Sift through your old photo albums, record or CD collection, or memory box or diaries and as personal experiences rise to the surface write them down in your notebook.

Lists are good. Find your notebook and pen and prepare to make some lists.
If you did the following with a writing friend or at a writers' group you would
find that some of you would have listed the same items. This doesn't mean
you had the same personal experiences but it does mean that you have life
experiences in common with others. This is often the reason work sells.
Whatever it is, readers can associate with it, relate to it. They think that
whoever wrote it understands them.

Now, just like school – remember spelling tests you had? – write numbers 1
to 10 down a page of your notebook. Do it four times.

Thinking carefully list the following:

- Ten *happy* occasions in your life.
- Ten *sad* times.
- Ten *interesting* people.
- Ten *interesting* places.

You could take one item from each of those lists and use them to write a
story.

- The happy and sad occasions help with plot.
- The people are your characters.
- The places are your settings.

One or more of the happy events might make a letter or short article. The sad
things could be written up to suit a tabloid magazine or used as a basis for
fiction. The places might make a travel feature. They could inspire you to use
them as a setting for a story, or even a novel.

When you have time you could explore each item on your list. Perhaps one of
the happy times you experienced was the day you realised you had fallen in

love. Imagine exactly how you felt, your physical feelings, your emotions, what the day was like, bits of conversation. If you write a page or two, or even a paragraph or two, then you can return to this whenever you need to write a happy scene. It will remind you of exactly what falling in love feels like. It will take you back to that time and allow you to, once again, feel that way. You will be able to read it, remember it and use your own personal experience of falling in love to write a fictional experience. Different characters, different setting but the same feelings.

If you have to write a sad scene revisit a sad time in your life. It will be in your notebook of personal experiences. Allow yourself to explore that sadness so that you can more easily write about grief or pain.

If you are stuck for ideas take a look at your interesting people and places. One of the people you have written about could become the main character in a story or novel. Or you could mix two or three of them together to make one new person.

If you are the sort of writer who begins with a setting then re-examine your list of interesting places and see if one of them sparks your imagination.

WHAT TO DO WITH YOUR PERSONAL EXPERIENCES

Your personal experiences can be used in whatever you write. Draw on your own life in order to write fact or fiction. Here are a few of the subjects which will be covered later in this book.

- Take your boss and your best friend and create a new character.
- Sell one event in your life to several markets.
- Impart knowledge you didn't think you had to readers who didn't think they needed it.
- Put bits of yourself in fictional stories.

◆ Use personal traumas as fiction or non-fiction, or both.

How to use one personal experience for several markets

Some personal experiences will only make a letter. Others may be suitable for short stories, articles or both. You have to decide how much mileage any particular personal experience is capable of.

EXAMPLE

After an exceptionally high tide we discovered hundreds of starfish stranded on the beach. Five-year-old Dan began counting them. When I asked him how many there were he told me, 'Ten hundred thousand starfish'. It had to be the title for a story. Later that night he was counting the stars to see if all the starfish had gone to heaven. This experience could have made a letter complete with photo of the long bank of starfish. It was an amazing sight. It also had the makings of a picture book, but was written up as and sold as fiction to a women's magazine. It could also make an article but would need research as I know very little about starfish. Is this washing up and dying on the beach in their thousands a common occurrence? I hope not.

This was a tiny incident and is proof that you do not need to climb Everest in a T-shirt in order to sell your story. If we all had to wait for major events to happen in our lives then the pages of books and magazines would remain empty. With the right treatment, most personal experiences can sell.

Nothing should ever be wasted

As I was writing this an email arrived from short story writer, Paula Williams. She had broken her ankle and wrote:

'Had my new cast fitted yesterday. Not much improvement but I've now wedged a sock under the heel which seems much better! I'm going to write this up as an article called "Things they don't tell you about getting about on crutches". Nothing's ever wasted, is it?'

PROOF THAT YOU CAN USE ANYTHING

I was once unfortunate enough to get a boil on my bottom. It was painful and prevented me from sitting down for two whole weeks but I wrote about it and the piece appeared in two small press magazines as a warning to other writers.

— A WARNING TO ALL WRITERS —

Excuse me for tackling a delicate subject and such a personal one but I really think it should be aired. It's something not many people talk about and an item that, as far I know, has never been tackled in any How To Write book or article in any writing magazine. Consider this a first. Also consider it a warning.

Writers tend to sit around a lot. We sit and think. We sit and write. We sit and think about writing. Therefore shouldn't we take care of the seating department? I'm not talking chairs here. I'm talking bottoms. We never think much about them, do we? (Or maybe some of us do. There's a lot of erotic literature about and the Victorians loved well padded posteriors.)

In the final five weeks of last year I sat down to write my great commercial novel. I'd honed up on novel writing, done my research, planned my outline, knew my characters and was ready to go. In fact I managed 60,000 words. Now that's a lorra lorra words and a lorra sitting down. It didn't particularly worry me because I've always been a static sort of person, well suited to long periods of physical inactivity. But then, at my halfway stage, disaster struck in the form of an abscess on my right buttock. The squeamish should skip the next bit. It was as big as a saucer and gave off so much heat I could have roasted chestnuts in the leg of my knickers, that is if I was the kind of old-fashioned girl who wore knickers with legs in.

I spent ten days lying on my stomach, taking antibiotics and painkillers and being pestered by my minor characters demanding that my second best-seller (the second one in the six-figure, two-book deal I'm dreaming about) be all about them.

Occasionally I tried writing. Doing it in a prone position seemed to be the answer but I soon realised, with horror, that I'd virtually forgotten how to handwrite. Standing up was painful so that was also out of the question. Most of my time was spent thinking, making notes and phoning friends. And here comes the point. Several writer friends informed me that they too had suffered the very same malady when writing their longer works but they'd never warned other writers that this could happen. They'd never knocked off an article on Writers' Bum, the equivalent to Tennis Elbow and sent it off to a magazine. Apparently, women appear to be more prone to WB than men, probably because the female of the species is more sensitive. I reckon I must be a direct descendant of that Princess – the one who could feel the pea beneath the mountain of mattresses.

Allow me to suggest that, prevention being better than cure, we should all take a daily constitutional in future.

Stephen King used to be my excuse for not taking exercise – he was nearly killed by a truck whilst taking his daily four mile walk. Perhaps I'll try some local footpaths, as I don't want this experience again. They should be safe enough.

Anyway, let this be a warning to you. Please take this article seriously. I swear it wasn't written tongue in cheek.

OVERCOMING writers' block

Notice there are no capital letters for writers' block. Capitals would make it important, and it isn't. This condition is not one of my personal experiences. Is writers' block one of yours?

If you feel you are suffering then there has to be a reason. What you consider to be a 'block' could be due to one or more of the following:

- **You are stuck and feel you cannot move on from that place**.
  If a fallen tree had blocked the road you were travelling along, what would you do? Sit and wait for it to be moved? No. You would backtrack and find a way around it. You can do this with writing too. Either go back and find a way around, or leave that place and move to another where you are able to move from.

- **Self doubt has crept in and you have accepted that you cannot write**.
  Self doubt is what each and every one of us has had or will have at some point in our lives, and not only about our writing. Accept it as a normal part of life. Tell that little voice in your head to shut up.

- **You don't want to write, but won't admit it**.
  There are times when we simply don't want to write. Some writers can force themselves to produce the words – a journalist can't turn up for work and announce he or she doesn't feel like writing. The sun is shining and you would sooner be out in the garden. Go there. Give yourself permission and get it over with, and then return to your writing. Don't make excuses. Learn to be honest with yourself.

- **You assume you have nothing to write about**.
  The answer to this one is to go out and find something. You can leaf through your personal experience file and discover a subject, even if it is writing more about a memory you have listed. Later you might discover one or two good sentences, descriptions or analogies in this and they could be cut and pasted into a completely separate piece of work.

Or you can go and expand your file so that you do have something to write about. Add a new experience or place or person. Visiting a place you have never been to before will give you not only new scenery but new thoughts and ideas. You might meet new people there and be able to use them as characters. They might speak and provide you with a piece of dialogue that you can use as the opening line to a story.

EXAMPLE

I once spent several days in hospital and discovered it was the perfect way to find new ideas to write about. After five days I

♦ was brimming over with new experiences
♦ had heard enough dialogue to write a play
♦ had met enough strange, exotic, eccentric and altogether weird and wonderful characters to populate a dozen novels.

I returned home with a full notebook. In-between the regime of medication, meal-times, visitors and all the other day to day business, I recorded scraps of dialogue and character profiles, wrote a few fillers and even a recipe. On top of all that material I also had the actual experience of an operation and recovery which I could have written up and offered to one of the weekly tabloid magazines.

I sent a letter to a local newspaper about my experiences with the NHS – how there were no beds so I was taken to the children's ward to don my hospital gown. Then, because there were no trolleys I had to walk along the corridors to the theatre, carrying my luggage. This was Star Letter, the prize for which was a dictionary. It led to a phone call from a reporter whose account of my experience made front page news under the headline of 'Local Woman's Nightmare Hospital Ordeal'. I should have written it myself.

The woman in the next bed told me, during a conversation about her holiday, that there are 4,000 pleats in a Greek soldier's kilt and they have to iron them themselves. I am still trying to think of where that bit of useless information could be sent.

A stay in hospital provides the opportunity to mix with people you would never meet in your everyday life. From all walks of life – some you may not have known existed – these patients and staff provided me with characters. One was a compulsive eater. When she wasn't eating crisps it was chocolates, and her visitors arrived with parcels of fish and chips, brought in to fill any gaps she might have. Another was a glamorous elderly lady who never removed her huge dark glasses, and wore a green silk robe and golden slippers. She told me she had been a Bluebell girl. Then there was the woman who kept on and on about how wonderful her son was – but he never came to visit.

Some of the characters I met have made appearances in my short stories. Words heard in Ward 5 have been transplanted into my work.

Nothing that happened in that hospital was used immediately, apart from writing the letter that is still listed on the internet when I stupidly poured out my heart to the reporter. Not everyone wants to provide fodder for front page headlines but a lesson was learned. Here it is. If you are interviewed do not answer questions immediately. Do not respond with the first thing that comes into your head. Always pause before answering questions and give yourself time to think about what you are going to say.

When you have a new experience it immediately goes into your memory bank. You may not use it for a few days, weeks or even years. Then one day it surfaces and becomes a subject for you to write about. It is as if once placed there, at the back of your brain, your unconscious works on it and lifts it to the conscious at the right time.

Novelist Eileen Ramsay says, 'In winter the fields outside my house look very bare and barren, as if nothing is going on. Don't you believe it. An unbelievable amount of activity is taking place under the ground. It will take several months but boy, come up and look out of the windows by March. That's what writing is like. Accept the fallow moments. Do other things; your fingers aren't working but your head and heart certainly are.'

EXERCISE

If your fingers aren't working then what do you want to do? What ambitions do you have? Do you want to learn how to paint, to skate . . . What could you do today? This afternoon?

Think of experiences that you have not had before, however great or small they may be. Wear orange. Learn how to spit. Learn how to fly. Visit that castle.

Make a list of what you could do today. Try for ten ideas.

Make a list of things that need more planning, things you would like to do in the not too distant future. Try for ten.

PART ONE

Non-Fiction

2

Easy Ways To Start

Let's begin with little bits – pieces of writing that are composed of very few words. These can often be written as soon as a past experience rises to the surface of your consciousness, or a few minutes after you have experienced something to share.

WRITING FOR LETTERS PAGES

Nearly all magazines and most newspapers have pages, or at least a few columns, set aside for readers' letters. Look out for them every time you pick up a publication. See what is being offered for letters. Most of the women's magazines pay. Specialist magazines (such as those about gardening or other hobbies and interests) offer money or prizes, as do some newspapers.

Before you begin to write

Once you have your markets you need to check for the required length. Most of the published items will appear to be around the same number of words. Check out the longest and shortest items. Count the words used and stick to the length that particular market uses.

My first ever sale

The £2 I received for this letter, printed in the now defunct *Woman's Realm*, was the first money I ever earned through writing. Here's my letter:

We were watching seagulls by the River Severn in Worcester. 'They're a long way from the coast,' I remarked to my friend.

'Oh, it's not far if they come up the motorway,' came the reply.

That was the start of my writing career – a silly remark made by a friend as we walked across the bridge on our way home from work. A personal experience. As soon as I reached home I wrote it down. My first attempt at recording it came to nearly 100 words but magazine letters aren't usually that long so I cut it . . . and cut it . . . and eventually it came down to 35 words.

You could sell a snippet of conversation. If a friend says something funny be sure to write it down, before you forget it, and later turn it into a letter.

Read for ideas

As you read the letters which have been published they might remind you of similar experiences. Perhaps there's one about a childhood incident, say riding a bicycle for the very first time and it reminds you of the day you managed to roller-skate without hanging on to the wall. You could write down your personal experience of going solo on skates and send it in as a response to the letter you've seen.

Or you might want to reply to something someone has said. For instance, someone has written in to say they realised they had finally grown up because, after returning home from a shopping trip, they made a cup of tea instead of pouring a glass of cola.

Now you ask yourself, 'When was the first time I felt grown-up?'

Drift back into your past. When was the first time you felt grown-up? Write for five minutes NOW. Begin with – I knew I had grown-up the day... or, I felt grown-up the day...

WHAT YOU NEED TO KNOW

You can type or handwrite your letter. If you're going to be sending out lots – and some writers do – then you could alternate. There's no need to enclose a stamped addressed envelope unless it's specifically asked for.

Make sure your name and address is on your letter. Also check that you have given any other information asked for. Some magazines ask for your age and/or your telephone number.

When you begin to write your letter ramble as much as you like in the first draft. This way all the information you need will be there. Then start cutting out words. Do this by sticking to your subject and deleting anything which has nothing to do with it.

◆ Don't ramble.
◆ Stick to the point.
◆ Keep your sentences short.

EXAMPLE

Here is the first draft of a letter I wrote:

My four-year-old grandson, Dan, telephoned to give me explicit instructions on how the cake I'd promised to bake for his fifth birthday should look. 'I want a crocodile,' he said, 'with blood coming out of its mouth because he's eating a man.'

> What a challenge! I made a huge sponge in a roasting tin, cut it into shape, covered it in green marzipan and sat it on a bed of chocolate cream. The man's legs which stuck out from the croc's mouth were also marzipan. And the blood – raspberry jam.
>
> Dan and his party guests loved it and all demanded a bit with blood on! I'm dreading what he'll come up with this year.

As I had a photo of this amazing cake to send with those 116 words readers would be able to see exactly what it looked like, therefore some of the description could be cut. That Dan was four before his fifth birthday was obvious. That could be cut too. And this wasn't a recipe so the sponge, roasting tin and green marzipan weren't needed. Neither was the bed of chocolate cream.

Here are the 31 words which remained:

> This is the cake I made for my grandson's fifth birthday. Dan wanted a man-eating crocodile. The marzipan legs and raspberry jam 'blood' were very popular with all his young guests.

Taking photos

The good news is that you do not need an expensive camera and you don't need to be a professional photographer. Most of the pictures used are family snapshots – the sort of thing anyone could take with a cheap throw-away camera.

Before rushing out to take endless pictures it's a good idea to go through all your old photographs and see if there are any that could have a caption added or a few words written about them. This way you can get started right away.

You may already have something from when you looked through your albums and made notes in your Personal Experiences file.

Keeping track

You will need to keep track of the letters you send out. Send to one magazine at a time and wait for six months before sending the same letter to another market.

Use an exercise book or create a file on your computer and write your complete letter, or the gist of it, on the page. Then add the date and the magazine you have sent it to. If it's not used within six months you can then add the name of the next magazine, together with the date you send it out again.

Set aside the time to compose one, two or more letters each week. Your exercise book will soon fill, or your computer file grow, and you will have a constant supply of work out.

CHECKLIST – GOLDEN RULES

♦ Count the number of words used in the longest letter on the page you are aiming to write for. Make sure your letter isn't longer than that. Cut it down to size. Remove every unnecessary word.

♦ Keep sentences short and clear. Don't use clever words. For example, why say *purchase* when you can say *buy*?

♦ Check out all the magazines and always send to the highest payer first. There is no guarantee that your letter will be used by the first magazine you send it to so start with the highest payer, and if they don't use it you can send it to the next on your list.

- If you have a photo to go with your story, send it. Magazines use loads of pictures and you might stand a better chance of seeing your work in print if it's accompanied by a photograph.

Slightly bigger bits

Let's continue with slightly bigger bits. There are plenty of openings for your personal experiences. You could write about your holiday, your operation, the funny thing your child said. You could share some household or garden tips. But before you begin you need to conduct a little market research.

DOING MARKET RESEARCH

Discover who wants what by checking out a few magazines. Buy one of the weekly 'tabloid style' magazines. Or buy two, or half a dozen. Do not use old copies as the requirements may have changed.

Taking each one in turn begin with the first page, the inside of the front cover, and check to see if there are any openings for readers. They'll say something like this:

- £50 paid if we use your tip and photo.

- The day that changed my life. £30 for each story used.

- Household and garden tips – £50 for the tip together with a photo. £20 for tips alone.

- Useful, interesting or valuable items found at car boot sales – £30 for each story. Send with photo and phone number.

- If you have a beauty problem, ask us – £20 for each letter plus £20 for photos.

- My operation. (For some reason the general public are enthralled by stories of operations, especially if they go wrong!)

- Embarrassing or memorable moments – up to £100 paid.

- Naughty jokes – £15 for each saucy joke.

- Spooky stories – up to £50 for each experience used.

Get the idea? This selection was taken from several magazines. Requirements and the amounts paid change frequently so you must keep up to date. Check out a different magazine each week and try composing one piece of writing each time.

Keep turning those pages and make notes of all the openings on offer. Or tear out the pages that interest you and keep them in a box file. Look for anything that says '£x paid for readers' *whatever'*. These could be hints, tips, supernatural incidents etc. One thing you can rely on is that you will find some in your life-long collection of personal experiences. All you need to do is open your file.

If you research several magazines at the same time you will also discover that they pay different sums of money. Discover the best paid markets. If they do not take your offering then you can send it on to the next best paid market and work your way down the list.

Some will say, 'Up to £x paid'. That does not mean that they will automatically pay the top whack. They do mean 'up to'.

Before you begin to write

You have researched your markets so once again you need to

check for the required length. Some items may tell you how many words are required. With others you will have to count the words. Make sure you stick to the length that particular market uses.

Using personal experiences

My grandmother used to give me a packet of salt and send me out into the garden to look for slugs. Salt on their tails apparently made them curl up and die which was preferable to them gorging on her lettuce. How many ways are there to get rid of slugs? Do you have a more humane method? One gardening or household tip could lead to another.

How can red wine stains be removed from silk cushions? I don't know. Do you? Did you watch your mother or grandmother use their tried and tested method of stain removal?

Evoked by smells

Sometimes an experience, or memory, can be brought back to us by a voice or a smell, a picture or an item of clothing.

Participants at a writing workshop were asked to think of a smell which meant something to them. An elderly lady chose the smell of bacon and wrote a page about her childhood 70 years before when workmen had been cooking bacon over a brazier in the street and they had invited her into their tent to share their sandwiches. Imagine that happening now. They'd all be arrested! With a little prompting she remembered the heat of the fire on her face, the biting cold outside, the smell of tar, along with the bacon.

When I was a child my mother made apple pie every Sunday and we listened to the Billy Cotton Bandshow on the radio while we were eating lunch. For me the smell of apple pie and Billy Cotton's shout of 'Wakey Wakey!' are inseparable.

EXERCISE

Is there a certain smell which evokes memories for you? Choose one of the following and write about it NOW.

apple pie	fish and chips	perm solution	bacon
creosote/tar	garlic	lavender	gas
curry	petrol	fresh bread	wet dog
sherry	fried onions	humbugs	feet
mothballs	paint	smoke	seaweed
books	water		

Once you have completed your writing you may discover you have the makings of a letter. Play about with it. Move words around, delete some, get it into shape – and post it to your chosen market.

A delegate on a writing course chose to write about the smell of mothballs. It reminded her of how she used to help her grandmother push mothballs into molehills as the smell drove the moles away. Once home she found a molehill and stooped down by it to have her picture taken. A few weeks later she wrote to tell me a magazine had accepted her letter and photograph and were going to pay her £50.

OTHER OPENINGS

The day that changed my life. Have you had one? If so then you write it down. This is how to use a personal experience and sell it.

My operation. A good percentage of the population have had

some sort of operation. Have you had one? Did something go wrong? Did it change your life for better or worse? Think about it for a moment or stop NOW and write about it.

Have you experienced something paranormal? Seen a ghost? Had a premonition? Magazines will pay for your story. Just remember those golden rules:

- Count the number of words used.
- Keep sentences short and clear.
- Don't use clever words.
- If there's more than one magazine that could use that particular story then send it to the highest payer first.
- If the magazine uses photos send some to illustrate your story.

Opinion pieces

What gets on your nerves? What annoys you? Have a good moan about it in writing. Send it to a magazine or newspaper and see your complaint in print. You could also get a cheque or a gift for offloading your grievances onto the page.

Find the market, count the words and check out what sort of subjects have already been complained about. Irresponsible dog owners and chewing gum won't attract the editor's attention, not unless half the population stop complaining about them for the next five years, and that's most unlikely.

Think about social or moral issues, current problems in the news, ongoing problems on which you can add a fresh perspective. Do not complain about local issues to a national newspaper. If you are a grumpy old man, or woman, then write down your opinions about almost anything, and get paid for doing so.

TIP

Never read any newspaper or magazine without a pair of scissors to hand. Cut out any openings that you see and think you could use your personal experiences for. Then give yourself a deadline to write for that opening. Features are always changing and being replaced by new ideas so don't miss out by leaving it too long.

3

And My Specialist Subject Is...

EVERYONE HAS ONE

Everyone has a subject they can, or do, specialise in. Maybe you thought you didn't, but you'd be wrong. You may have several. Your specialist subject may be sitting in your Personal Experience file. If it's not already there then it will be by the end of this chapter.

You know more about yourself than anything else so your specialist subject will either be you or what you know.

What do you know?

We all have certain skills. Do you know *How to* fix a bicycle? *How to* get fit after a heart attack? *How to* use driftwood to make a garden seat? You must know *How to* do something!

INVESTIGATING MARKETS

The bicycle, the heart attack, the garden seat – all of them will fit a market somewhere but it's no good standing in a newsagents, however large it is, and searching the shelves. Only a small proportion of magazines published make it to those shelves.

Have you ever watched *Have I Got News For You*? This programme has a section where the teams playing have to guess the missing words from a headline. The headline will be from a well known newspaper or from a guest publication. When introduced the guest publication always gets a laugh because so many of them sound unbelievable, but they do exist, though they rarely make it to the shelves of retail shops. A friend of mine wrote for *Potato Monthly*. Now you don't see that in W H Smiths. So where can you find it, and other specialist magazines like it?

Go to the library and ask to see *Willings Press Guide*. It cannot be borrowed but you will be able to sit and look through it and research new markets, glean names and addresses of periodicals. National, daily and Sunday newspapers are covered as are all the special interest titles. And most of these will constantly be on the look out for material.

If you are a parent, then you are an expert on bringing up children, whether that is how to do it or how not to do it. If you're a good cook/gardener/home-maker then you are expert enough to supply tips about your expertise, if not articles or books. Whatever your skills or experiences there will be someone out there eager to read about them.

EXERCISE

Write down all the things you can do. You learned all these skills – from walking, tying your own shoelaces and learning to read to whatever it is you learned today. Perhaps you are good at organising children's parties or garden fetes. Can you make cushions, sweets, chairs or jigsaws? Have you ever learned to skate, fish, climb mountains, sail or fly?

This could prove a time-consuming exercise so list only what comes to mind now. You can add to your list as you read through this chapter.

You know far more than you realise and, written up in the right way and with a bit of investigation into markets that might be interested, you too could become an expert.

SPECIALIST SUBJECTS

Saving money or re-training

When a friend was going through a difficult time with finances she told me how she was coping with very little housekeeping money. 'I could write a book on 100 Ways with Minced Beef,' she said. She wasn't a writer so she never did write her book but she could have sent some of her advice out as hints and tips to women's magazines and earned some money in the process. She could have written an article on all the money-saving tips she was using. Later, she re-trained and landed a good job.

Does any of the above jog a memory for you? Has a money-saving tip you used surfaced in your memory? Did you re-train once the children had gone to school, or after you were made redundant? Write it all down in your file.

Magazines pay well for money-saving tips. If you have enough you could produce a book.

Articles on retraining or changing jobs later in life could be aimed at the 'grey market', those magazines specifically aimed at the over 50s. They could also be aimed at magazines for parents, especially mothers who could take distance learning courses at home while they are bringing up their family.

Mothers have lots of experiences to write about. How to amuse children without breaking the bank, how to cope with a naughty or destructive child, how to get children to eat a healthy diet. All these experiences could be offered to parenting magazines or written up for general interest magazines. And all would provide tips to be written in very few words for the weeklies.

Cheap travel and bargain places to eat out

My mother, living on a government pension, used her bus pass to the full. At least twice a week she would have a day out. A car-boot sale fan she would often show me her bargains. One was a huge tray of those little individual cartons of marmalade. For £1 she had enough marmalade to cover a year's worth of toast. She also knew all the cheapest places to eat well. I still have visions of her and her friend sitting with their eggs, beans and chips in a motorbikers' café!

Have you done any of the above? Are you on a pension? Could you write about the interesting and cheap ways retired people can enjoy themselves? Have you used your bus pass? What did you feel like the day it arrived? How many good deals are out there waiting for over 60s to enjoy?

Do you eat out regularly? Or use public transport to get about? Think of how many ways you could write up your experiences. But first write down any personal experiences that popped into your head while you were reading this section on cheap travel and bargain places to eat out. Add them to your file.

You can use these experiences to write dozens of articles. Why not aim them at the grey market? Readers on limited incomes would want to know the best ways of enjoying themselves without spending too much cash.

Local history

I met a man who knew all about the common he lived on. He wrote up everything he knew, then added some research material. There were only ten houses nearby so he had a copy of the history printed for each neighbour. Other people got to know and asked for copies. Then the local Tourist Information requested a dozen or so. When we met he had sold 10,000.

Do you know the history of where you live? A snippet will do. It could be the history of your house, street, village or town. It could cover the years you have lived there or a short stretch of time. Maybe there was a fire or a flood or a demonstration. Think back. Dredge up those personal experiences. Add them to your file.

There is no reason why you shouldn't produce a small booklet that will sell and keep on selling over the years.

Student life

When Adam Millward, was a student already selling short stories to magazines he wanted to be involved with the student newspaper. He approached his first 'news meeting' with some trepidation but, since seeing his first article in print, hasn't looked back:

'After a year of reporting, I decided I wanted to get more involved, so applied to become a news editor. Along with three other applicants I was selected, and suddenly I was thrown into a crazy schedule of story collection, allocation, sub-editing,

designing and on print days staying up to the early hours.

'It was while reading a national writing magazine one day that it suddenly struck me I'd never seen any features on student media. I immediately sent an email to the editor, who responded eagerly and later accepted an article describing a week in the life of a news editor. Subsequently, I approached another writing magazine, who were also keen, and after reworking the article I sold that too. Using that personal experience in my writing provided me with a route into two national magazines with which I now have an active working relationship.'

Adam concentrated on his experiences of being involved with student media but there are plenty of other subjects a student could write about. What it feels like to leave home, how to get a part-time job to fit in with studies, how to survive on a small amount of money, sharing accommodation with virtual strangers. Lump all these together and there could be enough material for a book. Individual articles could be slanted at different markets. An article entitled 'I'm All Right, Mum' could sell to a woman's magazine as many readers might have kissed their offspring goodbye as they set off to university.

HOBBIES

Your hobbies, past and present, could supply you with ideas for articles, or a short letter. Maybe you are involved in a sport, or your hobby is something less strenuous. Perhaps you collect things, make things, fly things, investigate things...

EXERCISE

List your hobbies and interests. Don't forget past hobbies, the ones you knew a lot about but have now given up on. With a little research or a refresher course, they would become inspiration for your writing. If personal experiences of how you won a time-trial, flew the model plane you'd made yourself or discovered a long lost relative are already bubbling through your head, then write them down NOW.

MORE SPECIALIST SUBJECTS

Cycling

When my son was 12 he joined a cycling club, not the touring variety, but the racing sort. Soon after, as his parents, we were asked to help out as marshals. Eventually we bought bikes and joined too. Then our daughter, realising the club was mainly made up of boys, decided to join. Because I realised there was so much material in this sport of ours I used it to write several humorous articles for magazines and then to write a book for young teens. I drew heavily on personal experience for all of this writing. In fact I actually rode a ten mile time-trial to experience what it was like.

The above means that, as well as cycling, my other hobby was writing. Later, writing turned into a full-time job and very often I find myself writing about writing (as I'm doing here!).

My first article about cycling was sold to *My Weekly* and was called 'And Mother Came Too'. It told of how I bought a bicycle and started to ride to work. I also wrote reports about time-trials for the local newspaper. There are specialist cycling magazines who like to hear from touring cyclists and publish profiles of well known racing cyclists. Cycling is 'green' too so articles about the benefits could be produced for magazines dealing with health or environmental issues.

There are several well known magazines about writing. *Writing Magazine*, *Writers' Forum* and *The New Writer* are the best known, but there are others too and all would be happy to receive an article which had something fresh and new to say about the art of writing.

Keeping fish

Linda Lewis began her successful and varied writing career by selling articles about a hobby that she hadn't initially chosen for herself:

> *'My path into writing full time began when I worked for an insurance company as an administrator. My boss thought it would be nice if we had a fish tank in reception. All very well, but guess who got lumbered with looking after it? It was a steep learning curve!*

> *'I soon fell in love with the hobby and started keeping fish at home. Later, when I started a writing course, my tutor insisted I write some articles before going on to stories and novels. All I could think to write about were my three glass catfish (Kryptopterus bicirrhis).*

> *'My tutor liked the piece and encouraged me to send it to* The Aquarist and Pondkeeper. *To my great surprise they took it. I went on to write dozens of articles for magazines both here and abroad. Now I write mainly fiction, but I still use fish-keeping as a theme every now and then.'*

More tips here. If you have information on how to look after any sort of animal, fish or plant then you could write out your ten top tips. Sell them separately or as one piece. Offer children's publishers outlines of books on the history or care of your chosen pet.

Walking

Simon Whaley has managed to combine his love of walking with that of writing. He says:

> *'At weekends, I used to slip across the M25 and escape the noise and bustle of Greater London by walking on the North Downs in Surrey. I find that walking is great thinking time for my creative juices. But I noticed that the walking magazines were lacking in routes for the south east (they had loads in the Lake District and the other National Parks) so I wrote up a walk I'd done and sent it in to Trail magazine. They published it, so I sent another one in. They published that too, and it all started from there. I now produce walking routes for* Country Walking *and* Country & Border Life *magazines and have written a book of walks too.'*

Walking is good for your health. As is cycling, running and any other kind of sport. Sell pieces to health magazines and women's magazines on your chosen subject's benefits to health and figure. Walking and cycling also provide the time to look at the scenery, the wildlife and the roadside flora. You could become an expert on wild flowers or badger setts.

Motorhomes

When Paula Williams's husband retired and bought a motorhome she initially didn't share his enthusiasm.

'I'd just begun selling short stories on a regular basis,' she says, 'so the idea of being away from my computer, for weeks at a time, didn't appeal. Technology came to my rescue in the form of a laptop computer, a mobile phone and a connection so that I can send and receive emails wherever there's a mobile phone signal.

'I love working at home but discovered that working on the move is equally enjoyable and inspiring. Several short stories have been triggered directly by the different people or places I've encountered during our travels.

'Last year I bought a digital camera and began exploring the non-fiction market by writing Site Reports for the motorhome/ caravanning press. They pay and don't take much time to write and – the big bonus – the editors got to know me and my work, so that when recently I pitched an idea to one editor for a two page article (with pictures) I was told to, "Go ahead".'

Site reports, articles on touring, tips on how to take care of your motor home or caravan, places to visit, sights to see, living in a caravan full-time – all fodder for articles and all with several markets available to the writer.

Genealogy
In 2002 after searching for over 30 years for her pre-adoption roots, Hilary Halliwell finally found her birth family via the Internet:

'During this hugely emotional time, a short story rejection arrived from My Weekly. *This rejection was different; they wanted to see more. Two months later I telephoned the*

magazine and, in apologising for not responding earlier, told them of my fantastic news. Much to my amazement, the editor suggested I write an article about my search and reunion with my birth family.

'I was terrified! But never one to be put off, I had a go and was delighted to hear from My Weekly, *within a few days, saying they'd like to publish the article in their "Your Own Page" slot.*

'Since then I have sold over 70 short-fiction stories and several articles to women's magazines. Several have been stories about adoption. Well, they do say, write what you know!'

And what you know is all down to your personal experience. There is currently a huge interest in tracing family trees as proved by several television programmes such as *Who Do You Think You Are?* I have heard of one man who discovered a great-great-grandfather had been hung for cattle-rustling. All families are unique and if you have uncovered the skeleton in your cupboard then write about it for the genealogy market, or slant it at a wider audience and sell it to a newspaper or general interest magazine.

COLLECTIONS

People collect all sorts of weird and wonderful items. Being minimalist at heart I have never collected anything, apart from books. My brother, as a child, collected stamps. An aunt collects thimbles, or is it egg-cups? I've seen a television programme about someone's collection of plastic carrier bags and actually it turned out to be very interesting. I've been in homes where collections of teddy bears, dolls in national costume, bicycle parts and theatre posters are on display (not all in the same place). I have been shown collections of letters, period costumes, walking sticks and stuffed animals. I've had lunch in a tea shop where the walls were covered in needlework samplers.

It would seem that almost everyone has a collection of well ...almost anything. You name it and someone somewhere loves and cherishes it. And somewhere there will be a magazine specialising in that certain object, or a general interest magazine that has a page dedicated to what people collect.

EXERCISE

List all the things you have collected during your lifetime. Did you begin with stamps, then trade them in for a train-set? Do you own a collection of powder compacts, candlesticks, or old newspapers? Begin with your earliest collection and work up to what you collect now.

Delve into the personal experiences your collection brings up. Which markets or shops have you visited in order to add to your collection. What about the auction sale you went to? It's not enough to list what you have in your collection. You need background information too. Use your own knowledge but make sure your facts are correct.

The history of your chosen subject, the famous people who have either made it or collected it themselves, where the public can see the National Collection – all of this can be included. Most of us know that a philatelist collects stamps, but what is the collector of photographs or plates called?

If you thought collectors of beer mats were probably called pub-crawlers you'd be wrong. They are tegestologists. An archtophilist collects teddy bears and a plangonologist, dolls. A copoclephile is a collector of key rings. Do you know the name for what you are as a collector? Linda Lewis's interest in fish means she is an icthyologist.

On an impulse I typed *National Collections* into an Internet search engine. It came up with 1,980,000 results. The first one that appeared was The National Collection of Phlomis (plants). By randomly clicking on a few pages I learned that there is a National Collection of Treasures associated with Robert Burns. Another of Welsh Photographs. Brogdale is the home of the National Fruit Collection. The British Lawnmower Museum has a unique national collection. Old Court Nurseries house the national collection of Michaelmas Daisies.

AND MORE SPECIALIST SUBJECTS

Buttons

You may think that your collection is of no particular interest to anyone – but you'd be wrong. Anna collected buttons. She could tell you where she got each one from, what it was made of, what age it was and what its history consisted of. She wrote about her collection and, over a period of years, it featured in half a dozen different magazines.

Now, what could be more ordinary than buttons?

Elephants and period costumes

Val Webster begins her article with one item in order to lead into her real collection. She starts with a question:

What constitutes a collection? Many years ago, I put three small elephants together on my sideboard. They had belonged to my mother and I'd played with them often as a child. I suppose I put them on view to remind me of my mother after her death. People saw them and made the assumption that I collected elephants. Now, many years later, I own more than a hundred elephants in all shapes and sizes – most of them gifts – and I've grown extremely fond of them. I wouldn't write about them, though and they were more of a happenstance than a collection. What I will put into an article is my wardrobe full of copies of period costumes and some very beautiful accessories – many of them genuine antiques. I didn't set out to make a collection of those either, but they do have a fascinating story to tell which is, in a way, my story too. From gorgeous fabrics, frills and feathers to bum-rolls and pocket hoops, they are all waiting for their five minutes of fame. Some items have had their share already – but that's part of the story I'm going to write.

The beginning of Val's article reminded me of my collection of pigs. Seeing one led to friends buying me others and a collection grew without me actually wanting one. I could not get rid of them and risk hurting the feelings of the pig-givers but I managed to dispose of them in a short story which sold to *Yours*.

Val's costumes could interest magazines dealing with history, sewing, fashion and dancing. A photograph of Val in Elizabethan costume could sell to one of the weeklies on their reader's page.

JOBS

What do you do for a living? Or what did you do before you retired? You may think your job is boring but it might interest other people. My most interesting job was when I worked for a company which put cameras down sewers and I typed the reports. Sewers began to fascinate me, especially the old Victorian ones

which were so beautifully constructed. I had always thought that
sewers were big enough to walk through. No. They come in all
shapes and sizes. Some are round, some oval . . . some are huge
and others tiny.

The equipment was interesting too – tiny moving platforms
carrying even tinier cameras. The workmen had stories to tell about
the items found in the sewers and how they once found themselves
surrounded by police because they had been reported as suspicious
when they were working outside a bank on a Sunday.

I have yet to write about sewers but they will undoubtedly turn up
in my writing one day.

EXERCISE

Make a list of all the jobs you have had. What did you do once you had left
school or college? Did you work part-time while you were still a student?
Have you been working at the same place for years? Or do you flit from one
position to another? Next to your jobs write down any funny personal
experiences that come to mind, or interesting information you were party to.

AND MORE SPECIALIST SUBJECTS

Education

Irene Yates, author of over 300 books, mostly educational, used
her personal experiences in teaching to write. This is what she has
to say:

*'When I was teaching one of my friends told me about a science
teacher at her school who had an article published in* Junior

Education. *I had always wanted to be a writer but until then it had never occurred to me to write anything about school. That night I sat down and typed up the poetry project I'd been doing with my class and sent it to* Junior Education. *They phoned me straight back, begging for more. A year later the Publishing Director phoned to ask if I'd write a series of book material for them. I told her I didn't know if I could because there were people more expert than I. Her reply was, "Yes, but they can't write. The way it works is, we publish your stuff and then you are the expert." So I did it. And from then on, I never looked back.'*

Apart from the market of educational books there are also educational supplements in national newspapers and magazines. You could also consider writing non-fiction books for children. (See fish-keeping.)

Fashion buyer

Rhona Taylor found a niche which allowed her to write about her job.

'I was a fashion buyer for our family business. Every week I read the Drapers' Record. *One year they asked for news from "your town". I sent in my first report about things that went on in the shop and they asked me to write each week. I did so for several years. My articles would appear as "News from Bourne-mouth;", "News from Liverpool", "News from..." all sorts of places that obviously never sent in any! I earned the princely sum of £8.00 a week less tax! I did enjoy writing and seeing my work in print. It all ended with my retirement in 1995.'*

Computers

Some years ago, Zoe King wrote a How To book – Cash from your Computer – which came more or less directly from her work in computers.

> *'I was one of the directors of a small photographic software company, and at the time, supplemented my income by doing design and layout jobs for people. Not many people had computers in those days so having not only the computer, but also the experience, gave me a considerable edge. I had written articles for newspapers and magazines for years, and it struck me that my work with computers could form the basis of a book. Coincidentally, I saw an advertisement from How To Books Limited in* Writers' News. *They were looking for new ideas for their series, so I contacted them, and with the help of an agent, worked up a full proposal, which was accepted. Twelve months later my first book was published, which opened many doors for me into the writing world.'*

The world of I.T. is always changing and therefore new information is needed by the computer and technology magazines all of the time. If you can write information in a simple and entertaining way then there are other markets to explore. The over 50s buy and work with computers but many are still dithering over taking the first step. You could persuade them to do this. Once again the personal experiences of knowing about this subject supplies you with the wherewithal to write ten top tips when buying your first computer, or tips on how to look after it.

You could be an expert and not realise it. Your job could become your specialist subject. If you've never considered this before it could be because your job is something you go to, and do, five days a week, and it has never seemed interesting enough to write about. Think again! Take a look at what you have written down for your last exercise and see if you have enough personal experience on a subject to become an expert at writing about it.

Whatever your sport, or whatever you collect, or whatever you do for a hobby, there will be a specialist magazine about it somewhere.

WRITING FOR DIFFERENT MARKETS

Write about your specialist subject and sell your article to a specialist magazine. After a quick look at one publisher's website I came up with the following specialist magazines: *Black and White Photography, Dolls' House, Furniture and Cabinet making, Carving, Woodturning, Wood-working*... There are magazines aimed at collectors of antiques, teddy bears, coins... Even cross-stitchers have a magazine dedicated to their art. Even what may be considered obscure interests have magazines or regular newsletters. There is a newsletter dedicated to the collecting of milk bottles. The pages of these magazines and newsletters have to be filled. Think about it. You could help.

Write it again and sell it to a **general interest/women's magazine**. It will probably need a lighter touch as you are not talking to fans here. You are speaking to readers who have probably never whittled a bit of wood or threaded a needle. Readers who gave their dolls' houses away when they were ten, dumped their old black and white cameras in charity shops and have never thought to examine a finely turned table leg. It's up to you to interest them. You might even like to begin with, 'If you've never thought to examine a finely turned table leg..'

EXAMPLE

I managed to combine both writing and cycling in one of my regular columns for *Writing Magazine*.

'When I'm not writing, I'm not writing and when I am, I definitely am.' It sounds straight out of *Alice in Wonderland* but is, in fact, something a friend said to me. And I know exactly what she means.

Hitting a dry patch means not a word gets written. This can last for a few days, weeks or even months but, once you start writing again, the more you write the easier it becomes.

My son was a semi-professional racing cyclist on the Continent. He trained 365 days a year. It didn't matter if it was raining or snowing or if he'd had Christmas dinner an hour beforehand. Out he'd go and put in the miles. If conditions were really bad he'd stay in his room, television on, pedalling his bike on static rollers.

One morning, after not writing for months, I announced I was about to start a book. At the end of that day my son had covered 120 miles and I'd produced nothing. My mood wasn't a happy one. My wail, 'I've forgotten how to do it.'

That's when he lectured me. How did I expect to launch into something big when I'd not trained for it? If he'd not been on his bike for weeks and then entered a 100 + mile road race he wouldn't expect to get anywhere. He'd not put in the training. After a lay-off in training he built himself up quietly, gently. A little bit of training to begin with and then he'd increase it every day. So, why didn't I do that?

'Think of writing as a sport and keep in training for the big event,' he said.

I'd end with 'out of the mouths of babes' but he's a foot taller than me.

ONE OFFS OR FOREVERS

Your specialist subject might keep you busy for years. Irene Yates has written books and articles, using her knowledge of teaching, for the past ten years. Once you have discovered what subject or subjects you can specialise in you may feel exactly the same way.

On the other hand you may think that you have only enough personal experience of your subject to write one piece for a specialist magazine, but the magazine in question could ask you for more work. If you've used all your personal experience and knowledge in that first piece then you will have to revert to research. This can be time consuming and the unwary often find themselves seduced by other subjects as they go along, using up even more valuable time. Yet research could make you an expert in a field which you previously knew little about and then you will have enough information to become a regular contributor.

Writing about being left-handed sounds as if it would have a limited market. Francine Lee says, 'I was made to write with my right hand when I first started school and had I lived in the 15th century I'd have been considered a witch. I'd always been interested in the quirks and superstitions associated with left handedness. With a bit of research on the internet and a visit to the library to confirm facts I had enough for an article for *The Lady*. I knew there was a Left Handers' Day sometime in August so it was written and sent out in good time for that.'

It is the final line that gives the clue to more sales. There is a Left-Handers' Day in August. It's an annual event so, with a little ingenuity, the same facts rewritten in a different way could be sent out to a new market each year.

Annual events

Are there any annual events you are involved with and could write about? Are there any you know the history of?

I have sold several pieces about Oak Apple Day which is on 29 May. On that day in 1660 King Charles II returned triumphantly to London after nine years in exile. Buildings and people were adorned with oak leaves which had been taken as a symbol of loyalty in remembrance of the King's best known and loved adventure, that of hiding from the Roundheads in an oak tree. In Worcester, known as the 'faithful city' the gates of the Guildhall are still decorated with boughs of oak on 29 May. It was from seeing the decorated gates that I was drawn into researching the history of Worcester. I wouldn't call myself an expert but I learned enough to sell several historical articles to a local newspaper.

FACTS

Facts are not copyright. They do not belong to anyone and we are all free to use them. Once we have produced an article using those facts it is the article that is copyright. No one else can use chunks of your article, word for word. That would be stealing, but they are allowed to use the same facts that you have.

4

Washing your Dirty Linen

According to the *Dictionary Of English Phrases*, by Albert M. Hyamson, F.R.Hist.S. and published by George Routledge & Sons, Ltd, New York, 1922, the phrase 'to wash one's dirty linen in public' means 'to publish in the course of a quarrel, that of which one should be ashamed'.

My grandmother would have seconded Albert, even though she would sit down once the Sunday roast was in the oven and leaf through the pages of the *News of the World* in search of stories concerning what she referred to, in hushed tones, as S...E...X. If she was alive now she'd be able to find S...E...X everywhere. Presumably 'Don't wash your dirty linen in public' is no longer relevant.

In Grandmother's day it used not to be done but now everyone reveals all. Once upon a time it was only the sex lives of celebrities and priests that made it into print. Now it would appear almost everyone is prepared to shout their secrets to the world. And if you can 'bare' it then you can make money via tabloid newspapers and the real life magazines.

UNDERSTANDING THE REQUIREMENTS

These are stories about ordinary people. They are not glamorous celebrities. They are the folk next-door who have a story to tell. Most of these stories concern relationships and problems caused by them, or relationships that have survived against all odds. The magazine markets dealing with real life want tales of great courage and bravery (see next chapter) as well as deception and infidelity. They, and their readers, want drama.

Washing your own

If you have a real life tale to share there are two ways to go about it. In many of the magazines there is a phone number to call or a form to fill out. You give the basic details of your story and someone else will write it up for you. If you want to do it yourself then you must study the magazine's style. Is it gentle or sensational? Tear jerking? Exciting? Once again you need to know your market before beginning to write. And, even if you think you have attained perfection and have given your chosen publication exactly what they are looking for, and they accept it, be prepared to see a different version when it gets into print.

I once gave myself ten out of ten for lurid only to discover that, when I opened the magazine to see my story, I hadn't known what the word meant!

Washing someone else's

If you hear a good story from a neighbour, a friend, anyone, then you could approach them and ask if they would allow you to write it for them. Come to an arrangement, and have this in writing, about splitting any money received.

A WARNING

Think before you leap. These publications nearly always ask for photos.

If you send one of your nearest and dearest in his Dolly Parton wig, best frock and stilettos, how are his workmates going to react? (Probably by photocopying the pictures, enlarging them to life size and using them to adorn the walls of the office/factory/wherever.) Are you prepared for your family to disown you when you tell half of Great Britain that you have been 'having it off' with your twin's husband/wife, or son/daughter or any three of those choices?

Even if your story isn't of the salacious type you should be sure that you want to do this before you begin.

WHY ARE YOU DOING THIS?

That's a good question to be asking. What is your motive?

Making money

It may be purely for the money. The real life magazines pay well and several hundred pounds could make a huge difference to your life.

Helping others

Perhaps you want your article to provide help to others who have undergone the same, or a similar, experience. This is a good reason for writing and publishing your personal experience but would you be prepared for it to lead to other things? Readers might contact you, via the publication you have written for, and want help or advice. Others might want you to form a self-help group. You should be aware that your experience appearing in a magazine could be the start and not the finish for you.

Providing therapy

Will the writing of this provide therapy in itself and you won't feel the need to share it? Writing can be therapeutic and, once your worries or secrets are written down, it could prove enough for you. The act of writing can provide healing, or help you get your problems into perspective. Once written you may want to destroy your work or the desire to share it could still be with you. Before sealing that envelope ask yourself – do you need an audience of readers or do you need counselling?

Taking revenge

Is this going to provide a form of revenge? Cheated wives spring immediately to mind here. Some have not only chopped the arms off their husbands' suits but have also sold the story complete with pictures of themselves wielding scissors. If you decide to spill the beans about your best friend's infidelity and how you had no idea it was your husband or wife who was the third point of the triangle you should ask yourself if seeing this story in full colour in a magazine which sells tens of thousands of copies a week would help you to feel better? It may only add to your problems.

Now ask yourself the following:

- Do you need a computer or do you need a therapist?
- Is your story going to inspire others, warn them or help them?
- Is it for your eyes only, those of a few close friends, or for a vast section of the public? It's up to you to decide.
- Is it going to open up old wounds and make you feel worse?
- Would this be catering to an obsession you have and won't let go of?

- Is this suitable stuff for sharing with the real life sections of the tabloid magazines?
- Would it be better for you to use your personal experiences as fiction?

When you opened the page to this chapter – Washing Your Dirty Linen – did an idea spring immediately to mind? If not there may still be some personal experiences lying buried at the back of your heart or brain. Ask yourself if you have anything that might suit the market? Have you done something you shouldn't have? Do you have a dark secret?

EXERCISE

Try the following to find out if you have personally experienced anything you could write about to suit the real life market. Write down as many of the following as you can think of.

- Incidents that scared you.
- Times you have been in trouble.
- Any rifts caused in the family.
- Any laws you have broken, including the Ten Commandments.

SEVEN DEADLY SINS

If that didn't do the trick let's consider the Seven Deadly Sins and see what can be made of them.

Lust

Lust sounds the most promising. Many real life stories involve lust of some sort, whether it be sexual, and sometimes mistaken for love, or lust as in an intense longing or craving. This could involve money and you might consider selling the story of how you were involved in the greatest bank robbery of all time or why you spent the Christmas club cash and let your friends down. Lusting after power does not appear as often, but come up with a good enough story... For blood-lust see anger unless you are confessing to being a vampire (and people have!).

Gluttony

Gluttony, excessive eating or drinking, could be confessing to an eating disorder, whether it be gorging on 40 bars of chocolate a day, compulsive eating, or at the opposite end of the scale, telling others of your personal experience of anorexia and/or bulimia. This subject would include alcoholism – How I Beat The Booze, or I Married an Alcoholic. And if you've ever been called a 'glutton for punishment' ask yourself why and if you could, or would want to, write about it. Battered wives or husbands, long-suffering spouses, men and women who have to put up with vindictive old relatives...

Sloth

Sloth actually replaced sadness as a deadly sin so think about both. First sloth, a lovely old-fashioned word for a disinclination to work. Laziness. Do you feel lazy? Is it psychological or do you have an allergy to dust-mites which prevents you doing any housework? In my opinion – and one of my specialist subjects is M.E. – after having two children who suffered from it – what was classed as 'idle-itis' a couple of generations ago could have been M.E. Was your sloth caused by a disease?

Sadness is normal but take it another few degrees and you could be writing about coping with depression or, and I hope not, your attempt at suicide.

Pride

Pride when it is reasonable or justifiable self-respect is fine. We should take a pride in our appearance, be proud of our writing achievements, our family's accomplishments (if you have any of these then refer to the next chapter, Wholesome Real Life) but some folk go overboard. When this happens their delight or satisfaction from owning a bigger house or better car than their friends and neighbours can get out of control. We all know the old proverb 'Pride comes before a fall' so if you have become inordinately proud of some achievement and then fallen you could write about it and add the published item to your list of things to be proud about.

Envy

Envy, jealousy, desire, resentment, spite... Like pride, envy is all right in small amounts. Let it get out of hand and you'll have something to write about. Were you ever so envious of a friend that you took something from them (like a boyfriend/girlfriend), or plotted their downfall? If you've ever said, 'I'm so envious of you,' did you really mean it? Why? Did you do something about it? Steal their work or idea and pass it off as your own? If you weren't able to curb your envy and you want to confess in public then what are you waiting for?

Anger

Anger is a powerful emotion. Think about the consequences of anger and where they could lead you. Anger could cause you to lose your family or even lead you into standing in the dock on a murder charge. Uncontrollable anger means violence, as opposed to justifiable indignation – which can also be written about. Have you been on an anger management course and, if so, why? And did it work? Who persuaded you to go there? Do you want to share your experience with others? Do you lecture on anger management? Could you, with their permission, use some personal experiences from your class?

Avarice

Avarice is classed as an insatiable desire for wealth or gain. Perhaps avarice led you into indulging into one or two of the other deadly sins. If you have ever been in that groove where you believed money can solve everything then perhaps you can turn your personal experience into money by writing about it – for wealth and gain.

And one extra for luck – revenge

Revenge isn't one of the deadly sins but the only reason I can think of for it not being included is that the Eight Deadly Sins doesn't sound as good. (No alliteration.) Revenge can get nasty but there can be a certain delight in wreaking it. We all know that revenge is sweet so are you plotting revenge on your husband and/ or his mistress, your wife and/or her lover? Did a certain person cheat you, make you look a fool, beat you to a promotion when they didn't deserve it? If you are still at the plotting stage you have nothing to write about – yet. If you have already taken your revenge now is the time to tell all.

LEARNING FROM SOAPS

Soaps, or as I and many others prefer to call them, Continuing Dramas, because both the writers and the actors should be admired for doing such a good job, know all about dirty linen. If it wasn't for the traumatic experiences their characters endure then the viewers would be switching off in their millions. Whether your favourite is *Coronation Street, Eastenders, Emmerdale, Neighbours* or any of the other continuing dramas, take a moment to consider recent plot-lines. Between them these shows have covered almost every subject under the sun – from adoption, through to murder and onto teens being zonked out by booze or drugs.

If you watch continuing dramas and find yourself saying, 'That happened to me too,' then you have a suitable story for a real life magazine. Drama is what the real life magazines want.

When an emotional or controversial subject is covered in a continuing drama, details of a helpline are often given at the end of each episode. These helplines often receive hundreds of calls from people who would not normally be brave enough to ask for help. It is because they have related to the character in the drama who is suffering that they feel able to pick up the phone and start their journey towards making the changes necessary in their real lives.

Your story could cause the same reaction. It could be the catalyst for someone in the same circumstances as you have been describing. They might follow your lead and find a way out of their situation. You would probably never know that this has happened but it would have been your personal experience that helped a complete stranger to turn around their life.

If this chapter hasn't had you scrabbling for pen and notebook so far, then try reading through the following A–Z with pen in hand. You will have personal experience, or know of someone who has experience, of at least one subject. Probably loads more.

AN A–Z OF IDEAS

◆ A for assault, abortion, Alzheimer's, anger
◆ B for bullying, bigamy, bulimia, breast-enhancement
◆ C for children as in can't have any, got too many, lost one. C is also for cancer, comas and chatlines
◆ D for drugs, debts, dismembering, disloyalty
◆ E for euthanasia, ectoplasm, escorts, electrocution
◆ F for fireworks, fraud, fertility problems, fat
◆ G for gigolos, glamour, gambling, gratification
◆ H for homosexuality, heroism, heroin and heroines
◆ I for identity fraud, incest, immigrants
◆ J for jobs, jail-birds, judgements, jury
◆ K for kinky, kleptomania, kidnapping, knuckle-dusters
◆ L for love, lotteries, laughing-stock, layabouts
◆ M for murder (obviously), miscarriage, masochism, melanoma
◆ N for nausea, nervous breakdowns, nightlife, nip and tuck
◆ O for overdose, operations, obesity, orgasms
◆ P for prostitute, Peeping Tom, perversion, phantom pregnancy
◆ Q for quadruplets, quits (as in getting), quack-doctors, quests
◆ R for robbery, rape, recovery, runaway
◆ S for sexual (anything...pleasure, abuse, deviation, crime...), stalking, sperm donation, stutter
◆ T for toyboys, temptation, transplants, tyranny
◆ U for ugly, unemployment, underground, upheavals

- ◆ V for varicose veins, vasectomies, vanishing, vultures (without feathers)
- ◆ W for work, war, write-offs, wrinkles
- ◆ X for xenophobia, x-rays, X factor and all things X rated
- ◆ Y for yobs, yawns, yearnings, Y chromosomes
- ◆ Z for zoo (obviously), zoom lenses, zizz (and, not to be beaten by the final letter of the alphabet) zonked

Real life stories for magazines

Let's look at some magazines that use real life stories. *Take a Break* immediately springs to mind but there are many others – *Real People, Best, Take It Easy, Pick Me Up* ... Next time you are in a newsagents take a look at the magazines on display and you'll soon know which ones you need to buy. How? By reading the 'tempters' on the front cover. Here's a selection:

My man went missing
My Dad got his final wish
My partner's deathbed confession
My boyfriend is younger than my son
This is the last time I'll see my kids
My husband had 800 gay love affairs

Making a start

If you decide your story subject would make good fiction, or you would feel more comfortable passing it off as that, then the subject is covered in Part Two of this book. If you are sticking with the truth, the whole truth and nothing but the truth, OK. Now you must decide whether you have enough material for a couple of thousand words or if it will make a book.

WOULD YOUR STORY BE BIG ENOUGH TO FILL A BOOK?

A magazine feature covers the main event. A book would also use the before and after. For instance, the *My husband had 800 gay love affairs* story was turned into a book. This began with the author relating stories of her childhood, how she did not have much schooling because of suffering from polio, how she grew up and married a local boy and was later divorced. She then went to live and work abroad and that is where she met her second husband, a very rich and powerful man. She didn't realise that he was gay, and this was at a time when it was still illegal. From being a poor little girl from the Welsh valleys she turned into being a rich wife who had homes around the world. What a contrast. The book explains the reasons why she held onto this life even after her husband had confessed about his real life to her, and why she eventually knew she had to leave him whatever the consequences.

Would your experience run to 1,000 words or 100,000? (More on this in Chapter 6.)

5

Wholesome Real Life

In the real life magazines it isn't all kiss and tell, or murders and unfaithful partners. There is a balance and many of the stories that appear are inspiring, heart-warming and comforting. Readers tell of how they survived against all odds, came to terms with the death of a child or other loved one, how they learned something which has made them a better person. The learning could be anything from learning how to walk or love again to learning how to cope with a trauma, disability or illness. These are the sort of stories that inspire others.

WRITING ABOUT REAL LIFE EXPERIENCES

Do you have anything in your life which would be suitable for the more uplifting tales in magazines? Do you have any true life experiences which would inspire others? Have you done something exceptional? Have you overcome the odds and achieved a goal, beaten death, survived a terrible accident? These are the sort of stories real life magazines want to see.

These stories have happy endings. A trapped child, or animal, has been saved. A miracle cure, or a miracle, has saved the writer or a close relative from death. Divided families are reunited. Adopted children find their biological parents. Many operations have healed the scars of terrible accidents or acts of violence. The writer has come through the experience and can look back at it when not only the physical scars have healed, but also the emotional ones.

What these stories have in common is emotion. They are tear-jerkers. They are stories about ordinary people tackling extraordinary problems and the problems are not always of their own making.

Your personal experiences do not have to be sex related or as dramatic as the ones in the real life magazines. They can be ordinary, or seem ordinary to you, and the good news is that there are many other markets that would be interested. Have you walked or cycled from Land's End to John O'Groats? Met a long lost friend on a beach when you were holidaying in the antipodes? Learned how to swim in a class for adults? Found a piece of jewellery ten years after you lost it?

You don't have to cover years of your life. You can take one event, one moment... Readers want to be entertained. And you want them to say things like, 'That happened to me!' or 'I could do that'. There will be something in your Personal Experiences file.

EXAMPLES

Patricia Maw wrote 800 words about her experience of owning and running a pottery. She has also written about how she dog-sits for friends when they go on holiday.

I wrote about finally meeting a pen-pal. She had contacted me, from New Zealand, after reading one of my stories in *My Weekly*. Twenty years later, when we finally met, I wrote up the experience and sent it to the same magazine.

Angela Lanyon sold a piece to *The Lady* all about quinces, even adding a recipe for quince jelly. We have quinces in our garden but, apart from enjoying the flowers, I had no idea what to do with the fruit and wasn't even sure if it was edible. The article made for interesting reading. I could picture myself making jelly, but in reality know I never shall.

Angela also produced an uplifting article about surviving widowhood. This not only told of her sadness at losing her husband but gave step-by-step advice to other widows on how to rebuild their lives.

What is ordinary, every day life to you could be of great interest to others.

In the following edited excerpt from his latest book, *Choose Happiness, Ten Steps to Put the Magic Back Into Your Life* (Aber Bio, Studymates), scriptwriter and author Steve Wetton tells how he had pitched half a dozen ideas to a BBC radio producer.

'I like your writing,' the radio producer at the BBC said. 'Your characters and dialogue in particular, but none of your ideas really grab me.' Then as I was going out of the door he said, 'Don't give up. I'll be happy to look at anything else you send.'

By then I didn't really want to talk anymore. The fare to London had been more than I'd expected and I'd had to get up at dawn to catch the train and was feeling just the tiniest bit fed-up.

I gritted my teeth and managed to say, 'I appreciate your encouragement but I have a full-time job as a teacher and a big family including foster-children and I need to sleep and eat occasionally...' and then I started out of the door.

'Hang on,' he said. '*That* sounds interesting.'

'Which bit?' I asked.

'All of it. A person who's teaching and trying to write but still has time to become a foster-parent. That was a really brave decision. Come back and tell me all about it.'

Incredibly this chance remark that I'd made led to me writing a 30-minute comedy drama series for radio about a couple who become foster-parents. It was called *Growing Pains*. Later on I turned this same idea into a 50-minute series, with the same name, for television. We did twelve episodes for radio and twenty for television.'

By drawing on his personal experiences of being a foster-parent to write *Growing Pains*, which starred Sharon Duce and Ray Brooks, Steve proved that the real life which was 'normal' to him was interesting and entertaining to others. Twelve million viewers tuned in which proves the point.

NOTHING MUCH HAS HAPPENED

Some people will tell you that 'nothing much' has happened in their lives. An 80-year old woman told me this at a talk I gave to a writers' group. 'Have you never danced naked on the town hall steps?' someone joked. (Now there's a story.)

During a coffee break I had a chance to talk to this lady and 'nothing much' turned out to be working in munitions during the war . . . surviving divorce when it was considered shocking, bringing up five children on her own whilst working at three jobs because she was too proud to take 'charity' (social security).

I hadn't been in any of these situations. They were new and interesting to me, normal and boring to the octogenarian. Many writers forget that what is an every day occurrence to them is a rarity to someone else.

One of Mike Swaddling's writing sidelines is going into residential and retirement homes and recording older people's personal experiences. He has used them to produce a series of reminiscence books using the title *Telling Tales*. This is what he has to say:

'I sit and talk to people individually, leave a tape recorder running, and then come home and transcribe the tapes, keeping as close as I can to their words so as to give the booklets I produce, authentic "voices".

'I introduce the idea to them in groups, and very early on in the talk I say to them, "I know what all of you are thinking – he's not interested in me. I've never done anything special, I've only lived an ordinary life." And my response is, "There's no such thing as an ordinary life. Every life is unique – only you have had the experiences you have had."

'I have interviewed elderly people who have maintained when they came in the room that they didn't know what they were doing there, but a little persistence on my part has uncovered such things as winning the George Cross in the war, fostering 32 children, escaping from the Nazis in Hitler's Germany, almost becoming the next Cliff Richard, and countless other stories.

'Whilst I think that the British are a modest race as a whole, it seems that it is particularly pronounced in that generation. The attitude that got them through the war was one of just getting on with it, downplaying your achievements and not drawing attention to yourself. The side effect of that is they genuinely don't think they've done anything special. I've managed to persuade a lot of them that they have. The most rewarding part of it for me is seeing their reaction when they see something

that's happened to them set down in print – it gives their life some real value.'

Have you danced naked on the Town Hall steps? No? So, what have you been doing all your life? Try listing the following:

◆ Any incidents that caused you to laugh until you cried.

◆ One or two occasions when you've been brave or witnessed bravery.

◆ All the times you have been proud of yourself or family/friends.

◆ Some special occasions in your life.

NOSTALGIA IS BIG

Articles, letters and anecdotes about specific incidents in the past sell. The so called 'grey market' is aimed at readers over the age of 50. There are several magazines published especially for this age group – *Yours*, *Saga* and *Choice* are the best known. With a little market research you will discover that these publications cover many subjects including nostalgic pieces. You don't have to write about your entire life. A single episode is usually what is required. Try linking your piece with a particular date. Why not let everyone know what you were doing...

◆ the day the war ended
◆ the day the King died
◆ the day of the Coronation.

If you jitterbugged during the blitz, worked in munitions, saw The Beatles before they were famous... Think of the stories you tell your family and ask yourself if they shouldn't reach a wider audience.

(not necessarily for the over 50s)

Begin with 'I remember when...' and carry on from there, recounting any story from your past, whatever your age.

USING HUMOUR

My first dozen sales dealt with family life. I was a young wife and mother bringing up two children, working part-time, running a house... All my personal experiences at that time were of the domesticated variety and, when recounting them, friends would laugh. One day, whilst reading a woman's magazine, I discovered a funny article very similar to some of my stories. I studied it for length and style and sent off one of my own experiences. It sold. I sent off more. I wrote about family holidays, the chaos of getting everyone off to work and school whilst the cat was being ill and the son was prodding at the innards of the plugged-in toaster with a butter knife. Door-to-door salesmen, school plays and birthday parties all became experiences to write about.

The children came home and said silly things. They were sold to the Letters Pages.

Leanne looked admiringly at her brother when he told her he was going to sing solo in the school play. 'What, all on your own?' she asked him.

There are still openings for those of us who have a humorous outlook on life. Many of my sales dealt with tales of woe. There was the period when money-making was at the fore and I tried to grow mushrooms and earn a fortune (the newspaper advertisement assured prospective purchasers that they would). There was the stall at the flea market, the button-making industry. These all turned out to be disasters. The cat had kittens in the mushroom compost, we spent more at the flea market than we took, and my home-made buttons all crumbled in the oven. I wrote and sold each disaster.

WHAT CAN'T YOU DO?

If you have tried to do something and made a mess of it then write and sell the experience. Readers like to know there are others out there who can't wallpaper their own homes, grow vegetables successfully, bake cakes which actually rise.

If you later became an expert then include that. When we bought our motorhome we hadn't a clue about the camping and touring life, had no idea what all the pipes and plugs were for and had never been on a campsite but, after three months on the road, we became experts. I could write about that, and probably will. What could you write about?

EXERCISE

Think back to the mistakes you have made. What can't you do? List everything you can think of, no matter how small. Several small events can be fitted together.

Did the pleats of your skirt fall out of the waistband as you did a twirl on the desk in a sewing lesson? Mine did. I added that experience to a host of other sewing catastrophes and had enough for 1,000 words. Did the shed you took all day to construct lean 45 degrees to the right as soon as you turned your back on it? Add that to several other DIY experiences and write up your article.

These articles could sell to a general interest magazine, if they use humour, or a specialist magazine might consider them as a little light entertainment for their knowledgeable readers.

Don't forget your specialist subjects

Remember those lists of skills, hobbies, interests, collections and jobs? Don't waste them. Write them up for specialist magazines and then rewrite them to suit general interest magazines. Many women's magazines are interested in what their readers get up to. If you've made a quilt and it's in a display or has been auctioned for charity then you have the sort of story a woman's magazine might be interested in. Think of how to present your article. Would you go for the raising money for charity angle, the history of the craft, or about the display – why it has been set up and where it will be available next?

EXERCISE

Take a few items from your lists and see how many writing angles you can dream up for them. You have the knowledge. Don't waste it. Why not try to sell your subject in several different formats to several completely different magazines?

WRITING ABOUT CHILDREN

Hands up if you are a parent. Parenting is a tough job. It's unpaid, often unappreciated and there are no qualifications needed. Books about parenting, especially about babies, are popular. There are magazines dedicated to bringing up children. Why? Because at some time or another every parent has wished there was a manual about the job. Articles have covered every stage of a child's life but no child, parent or set of parents are the same which means that your article about encouraging a child to eat anything green is not going to be a carbon copy of mine, or any other parent/writer's. All of our parenting experiences are unique because of the unique child and the unique way we cope with them.

If you work, or have worked, with youngsters, your experiences would be of interest to others who are facing the same problems or, occasionally, joys. My husband once worked with homeless 16–25 year olds. His experiences range from depressing to inspirational, but he doesn't write. If you've done the same thing you will have the advantage. You write so it's possible for you to produce those depressing and inspirational articles. Balancing the two will give a better picture and the reader will stay with you. Concentrate on the depressing and you'll lose your reader. We all need hope in our lives.

EXERCISE

Make a list of all the problems your offspring caused you. Now make notes on how you tackled each situation.

WRITING ABOUT ANIMALS

Have you worked with animals? Do you own a pet? You can keep a dog to work on the farm, or as a pet, or to show. You could sell a picture of your cat playing with spiders made from pipe-cleaners. You could write an article about how you found your pet and what its character is like. You could also write a well-informed piece about the history of the breed.

I sold an article on how we chose our puppy and how he was partial to purple pansies. He ate them but left all the other colours alone. A friend sold an article about his dog's behaviour on the bus. The dog would beg for sweets from the other passengers. Another friend took a photo of an owl, which was with its owner outside a pub, and sent it to a magazine. Even if your pet is a goldfish you probably have a story about it and, whatever your pet happens to be, there will be a magazine wanting to hear about it, its exploits, history, and tips on caring for it.

WRITING ABOUT PSYCHIC EXPERIENCES

Have you had a psychic experience? Seen a ghost? Predicted a disaster? Visited a haunted house? Or lived in one? If you said yes to any of those questions then you are not alone. Take a look on the newsagents shelves and you will find a selection of New Age/ Psychic style magazines. They are usually published on a monthly basis. They offer advice from psychics, astrologers, complementary therapists and experts on feng shui, ghosts, dreams and auras. They also include real life stories from their readers. These range from a few words to double page features and are similar to the weekly real life magazine stories – but they have an added extra. Often this is a message from beyond the grave, a clairvoyant incident, an extra-sensory experience which enabled the writer to make the right choice when they were at a loss of what to do next.

When my husband had a severe heart attack and was struggling for survival we both had the same experience. At home, the phone woke me from a dream in which dead relatives were standing around his bed. As the nurse was making that call my husband saw his father and brother at the foot of his bed.

That's a quick outline. By the time I had filled in all of the details I had enough for a double page feature. The story was true, though many won't believe it. If most of your friends are the down-to-earth types who consider all 'that kind of thing' weird then you may not want to reveal a true story like that to them but they do not make up the readership of these magazines, do they? You could sell your story knowing that they won't see it in print, unless you choose to show it to them.

If you have had a similar experience to mine but don't want to admit it, then it can always be used as fiction.

6

Everyone Has a Book in Them

WHO IS IT FOR?

It is said that everyone has a book in them. Yes. It is the story of their own life. This has to be the purest form of writing using personal experience but, before you begin, the question to ask is, why would you write it? Would you write your life story

- for a wide audience?
- for the grandchildren?
- as a social history?

Writing for a wider audience

Once you know who your reader is going to be you will know whether this story of your life is to sell or not to sell. Finding a publisher is going to be difficult, unless you're a celebrity. To stand out amongst all the other autobiographies your life would have to include something special or amazing that the media could pick up on. If you ever make headlines on the national news, for whatever reason, then you should immediately be offering your life story to publishers. One event such as 'I tackled armed bank robbers' could be stretched into a book by giving information as to how you were brave enough to tackle armed men. You could include your upbringing because somewhere along the way you developed a strong sense of justice.

Take a look at the autobiographies currently being published and see how the writer used one big event in their lives from which to launch their whole life story.

Deciding to self-publish

If the mainstream publishers show no interest and you have faith in your book you could self-publish. This method is becoming easier, cheaper and more popular but there are questions to ask before taking the self-publishing route.

◆ Who will buy my book?
◆ Am I a good enough salesperson to go out there and sell it myself?
◆ Can I afford the money to put into this project?
◆ Can I afford the time to put into this project?
◆ Is it really good enough to spend money and time on?

That final question is a difficult one. You need to be very honest with yourself in order to answer it. Self-published books range from dazzling to dismal. Some writers unfortunately don't know the difference. My personal experience of one self-published writer is that of hiding in shop doorways when I saw her coming because I did not want to waste good money on her latest dreadful self-published offering. I also did not want to hurt her feelings by refusing to buy her book. She was an acquaintance, not a friend, so imagine how difficult it might be for friends to give you the unvarnished truth about your work. In most cases they won't. The brutal truth is they will tell a white lie in order not to hurt you.

Make sure your work is interesting enough to read and it is well written. Don't trust the opinions of friends and family. They tell white lies and are unlikely to be experienced in critiquing written work. Ask the opinion of an expert. If you're going to be paying for the publication then the extra money spent on a professional critique would be well spent.

Writing for the grandchildren

If your life story is going to be for your grandchildren then your style will be different. Chattier. Think of it as a long, long letter and use the same chatty style. Write down amusing anecdotes, funny stories and all that 'olden days' stuff that children and grandchildren love hearing about.

Today's children find it difficult to imagine life without telephones, televisions, computers...I remember when we were the first family in our street to have a fridge. My brothers and I used to fill up the ice cube tray with orange squash, add a cocktail stick to each cube and freeze them to make lollies. It was our first business venture. All our friends used to queue up to buy our home-made ice lollies.

By recording your life in writing for loved ones it will become more of a memoir than an autobiography. You can add bits as and when they surface. It will also become part of social history.

Writing social history

Social histories provide information on class divisions, work divisions, information about living conditions, healthcare, transport, infrastructure, establishment, foundations and structures. In other words, your personal experiences. It also includes background on particular environments or places, it shows how things came to evolve and change, and how people made a difference.

Everyone is a part of social history but only a few write down their experiences. If you were researching what it was like to live in a slum in a poor area of Birmingham during Victorian times you would need to research some social history. If you read several accounts of that period using reports from people living in different environments and from opposite walks of life you would see patterns emerging. You might have a woman recounting her story to a local historian, telling of her life in a back-to-back terrace where many families shared the same lone water tap in the yard, and the same toilet. At the very same time the folk at the other end of town could be holding fancy parties, having exquisite dresses made for them and riding around in fancy carriages.

Social history is all about personal experiences.

WHERE DO I BEGIN?

You return to the beginning of this book, to the place this question was first asked. If you completed the very first exercise you will not have a blank page with which to begin your autobiography. You will have your first memory. And there is more information to use. It will already be in your file of personal experiences. Move on from there to your memory aids – photos, diaries, memory boxes, music . . .

Whether you are approaching your teens or your 90s you have all those years of personal experiences to put in your book and the longer the life, the more material (personal experience) you have . . . There will be many years to cover, many joys, dramas, traumas.

Getting started

One of the hardest parts of writing is getting started. A blank page or screen is not a good beginning. However, if you begin with the first exercise in this book, *Write about your earliest memory*, you will have your start. There will be no blank page for you. Add to that everything in your Personal Experiences file and you may discover that you have already written a couple of thousand words of your life story. Simply carry on from there.

Writing the rest

How to write the remainder? Do not allow the task to overwhelm you. There are choices for you – differing ways of tackling this huge subject of autobiography. Which one you choose depends entirely upon what type of person you are. This is your life and it is you who is writing about it. You get to choose the method of collating your material. Below I have listed several methods. You could choose one or mix a few, or try them all.

♦ **Try writing in chronological order**. Begin with the first exercise in this book: *Write about your earliest memory*. If you are practical and methodical then this method could work for you.

♦ **Try listing major events and giving them dates** – births, deaths, marriages, wars, accidents, divorces... The gaps can be filled in later.

♦ **Try going through life a decade at a time**. Write down your decades and then add notes to them as and when the memories come to you.

♦ **Try chopping your life into ages**. Your first memory could stem from when you were three. What happened when you were four? Five? Carry on until you are up to date. This way you can leap from being six to being sixty.

♦ **Try cataloguing your life in sections**. What happened in the years before you started school? Next come school years – infants, juniors, senior, or whatever they were labelled when you were a schoolgirl/boy. After that comes work and family, different jobs. Maybe up until retirement, and after retirement.

♦ **Try hopping about**. Write down bits as and when the memories surface. Keep them separately and when you have enough, collate them into date order.

Finding a publisher and self-publishing

Whole books are written about these subjects. The writing magazines regularly contain articles on them. This is when you have to do your research. Compare companies. Ask other authors for advice and if you decide to self-publish work with people you feel you can trust, or publish with a company that has been recommended by someone you trust.

HUMOUR AND YOUR LIFE

Fred Secombe, Gervaise Phinn, Mark Wallington, Deric Longden and Peter Kerr all adorn my bookshelves. All have written books using their own life experiences.

♦ Fred Secombe's books are entertaining accounts of his life as a vicar.

♦ Gervaise Phinn is well known for his laugh-out-loud stories concerning his job as a school inspector.

- Mark Wallington took his dreadfully behaved dog on long distance walks and wrote hilarious books about them.

- Deric Longden has written many books using his personal experiences. Several have been made into films for television.

- Peter Kerr wrote about moving from Scotland to Mallorca where he worked on an orange farm.

AN ORDINARY LIFE

You do not have to be important or well known to sell part of the story of your life.

Publishers may not want your whole life, from birth up until now, but search your past, or your present, and see if there is something you can write about. I repeat, *what is everyday to you could be of huge interest to others*, especially if you can write with humour.

Using personal experience and humour

My friend, Phyll Handley, once worked as a gas meter reader. She told comical stories about her job, the houses she visited, the weird places some of the meters were in and the tales of some of the more eccentric people she met. Phyll added, 'Don't forget me stepping over dead rats in the cellars of the High Street restaurants after a regular visit from one of the council rat catchers. In all fairness they did come with a supermarket carrier bag and collect them up. But why was it always my luck to get there before them? Oh well, it was all in a day's work.'

And that's what our daily job means to most of us – a day's work. It is something we do all of the time. We may entertain our friends and family with anecdotes from our working life but the thought that we could entertain tens of thousands does not occur to us.

I do not relish the thought of reading meters in dark damp cellars where cobwebs stick to my hair and spiders wait to pounce, but that doesn't stop me enjoying my friend's stories from the days when she worked for the gas board. If she wrote a book I would be first in the queue to buy it.

To stay fit we are all supposed to clock up 10,000 steps a day. I have a stepometer and on only two occasions have I managed 10,000 or over. 2,000 is about my average. I don't enjoy walking but it didn't stop me from enjoying Mark Wallington's account of tackling the Cornish coastal path or the Pennine Way.

People are interested in people

These are the words of Cass Jackson and they provide the answer as to why readers buy books about other people's lives.

> '*Little of the material of which my stories and articles are fashioned is exciting or sensational. It is as available to you as it is to me. People find it interesting because they can relate to it. People are more interested in people than anything else in the world.*'

Yes. People are interested in people.

Peter Kerr and his family returned to Scotland after spending what he describes as 'three hectic, at times traumatic, but more than anything thoroughly enjoyable years *trying* to make a living growing oranges in Mallorca'. Peter says the most asked questions were, Whatever made you do a nutty thing like throwing up everything you were familiar with in the UK and hauling your wife and kids off to Mallorca to *try* and make a living growing oranges – something you knew absolutely nothing about? When you got there, how did the local country folk regard you? Did they think you were nuts? How did the kids settle into a new school in a foreign country? Did the kids think you were nuts? How did you cope trying to communicate with the locals and conducting business in a foreign language? Did the things you came out with make the locals think you were nuts? How about the strange food (snails?!), the mozzies, the *mañana* attitude towards everything, the incessant sunshine, the doctors, toothache, taxes, missing friends and family, missing *proper* beer and fish and chips? At times, did even *you* think you were nuts?

'Everyone wanted to know everything about everything,' he says, 'and so repetitively that I eventually decided to try writing down the answers in narrative form. And that was the start of my first book, *Snowball Oranges*. It took me two years to complete, and another eight to get published. Patience is not just a virtue, but very often an absolute necessity for an aspiring author. It certainly was in my case.'

Snowball Oranges was a success and Peter's time growing oranges in Mallorca provided enough material for four successful sequels. He is now classed as Scotland's top travel writer.

If you consider yourself ordinary, think again. What could you write about using personal experience and humour? Which part of your life could be turned into a book? Your job, home, hobby, interests, travels? What were your specialist subjects? (See Chapter 3.)

My mother was a home help and has always said she could write a book about it. She's got some good stories.

- The 90 year old who was being interviewed by the police as she'd reported seeing a streaker in the park opposite. (When the police asked her to describe him she said she hadn't looked at his face!)

- The woman whose front room she spring cleaned only to discover the following day that the old lady had stripped down an oily lawn mower in it.

- The lady who kept a stock pot in which she deposited any scraps. 'Dig deep,' she'd order as Mum ladled out her lunch. One time she found a fried egg in the bottom of the saucepan.

- The man who helped her make his bed and teased that 'couples who make a bed together end up in it'. He then said he wanted to show her something, promptly dropping his trousers to reveal an artificial leg.

Those four episodes could make four chapters.

EXERCISE

If you are already thinking of your days as a bus conductor or your experience of living in a poky bed-sit start making notes NOW. List three episodes (as in 'an ordinary life?'). If three are easy to think of, then add more. If you can list ten then the outline for your book is already written.

LIBEL AND HOW TO AVOID IT

When writing about your own life it is impossible to keep others out of it. Many of your friends, family and acquaintances may be pleased to see their exploits, along with yours, in print. Others may not, especially if you make them appear stupid, evil or anything else that will lower this person in the estimation of others. That is classed as libel which is a difficult subject. If in doubt, seek professional help. Ask a solicitor or *The Society of Authors*.

Using faction

This could be your solution. Faction is a mixture of fact and fiction. It allows you to write about events and experiences which actually happened, but characters are disguised, names changed, locations moved and dates changed.

INTERESTS – EXPLORED AND UNEXPLORED

If you've sold a couple of articles on your Specialist Subject then do you have enough knowledge to write a book?

When my tester was asked what sort of books he could write he came up with three work-related ideas. He had lots of funny stories about his time as a mobile motor mechanic, later in life he had several changes of occupation which were scary at the time. 'But if I can do it,' he said, 'anyone can.' And he could tell them how to. Now he has retrained as a reflexologist and wishes he could write as he would use this therapy as his subject and include lots of the personal experiences of his clients (case studies), with their permission, naturally.

Discussing this together we realised that, if he was a writer, he could also write a book about surviving a heart attack. The heart manual that was given to all the men in the coronary care unit was so heavy that, in the early post-attack days, every one of them had problems lifting it. It was written in a simple style and had cartoon illustrations but it missed out on the personal experiences of heart attack survivors and those of their loved ones.

People are interested in people. My tester wanted to know how other men had coped in this situation, preferably through upbeat stories offering hope, telling of complete recoveries, sufferers who were now running marathons... That is the way he would write his book, if he could. If you are reading this book because you are a writer, or you want to write, and you've had a similar experience, then you can write the book.

Writing how-to books

People want to know *how to* do all sorts of things – surviving that heart attack, starting up a business, planning a round-the-world trip, making life more bearable for a housebound relative. The list is endless.

Go back to Chapter 3 and the exercise listing the skills you have acquired during your life. Did you explore these enough to write an article or two? Could you expand on them enough to produce 50,000 + words? Could you tackle a book which gave hope to other sufferers of whatever disability or illness you have personal experience of?

Depending on what type of book you are tackling, your own personal experience may only be the basis of the work. You will need to research what you are writing about, find out about any help available and research statistics. (e.g. How many battered wives are living in refuges? How many children are born each year with spina bifida?) Your original idea will be only the tip of the iceberg. But by the time you've completed the task you set yourself you will undoubtedly have become an expert on the subject, and this could lead to other things.

Could you write a book about what you do, or did, for a living? Or one about your hobby? What specialist subjects are on your lists? Can you make a book out of any, or several, of them? Hobbies? Jobs? Lifestyle-changes?

EXAMPLE

Cass and Janie Jackson confessed that though they'd been working together for 15 years, the idea of writing from personal experience had never occurred to them until 2000. 'We'd always been interested in off-beat subjects like Reiki, astrology, crystal healing and so on. One day, when we were telling friends about a psychic fair we'd attended, one of them said lightly, "You know so much about all these things, you ought to write a book about them."

'Wow! What an idea! But would it interest a publisher? Amazingly – yes! Five years and fourteen books later, we realised that this stray comment led to the biggest writing success we'd ever had. Our books have been sold world-wide – and we still have more to write.'

A little inspiration

Cass and Janie's story should inspire you. They would be the first to tell you that if they can do it so can you. Don't claim 'Nothing ever happens to me'. Make a list of what *has* happened and you'll discover that you have material for all sorts of articles and books.

Writing local interest books

Whenever and wherever I go on holiday I always buy a local interest book. Books on pirates and shipwrecks, local walks which often include views to look out for or the history of interesting buildings passed along the way. There are always books on local history, myths and legends, ghosts and murders.

Mainstream publishers hardly ever touch this type of book as they are of local and not national interest, though there are exceptions. Small firms in the area you are writing about, and self-publishers, are your best bet. Take a look at the names of the publishers of the books that are available in your library or bookshop.

A novel will sell for a short while, then sales dwindle and eventually your novel goes out of print. This doesn't happen with local interest books. They can sell indefinitely.

Who buys them? People like me – visitors to the area. They are also bought by the people living in the area you write about.

We are not talking about dry academic accounts here. The most popular of local interest books impart information and facts but are written in an entertaining way. Anything of local interest can provide suitable material. Is there anything in your file of personal experiences that you could use? Did you work in a shop, office or factory that was, or is, a local landmark? Is one of your specialist subjects researching the paranormal? Perhaps you know all about ghostly goings on in your town, village or pub.

Before you rush off to put words on paper it's a good idea to check if anyone has beaten you to your chosen subject. A little research is needed here to find out what titles are already on offer and which subjects have already been covered. The places to check out are Tourist Information Centres, local bookshops, libraries and museums.

If someone has got there before you and your subject is covered ask yourself if you could treat the whole subject in an original way. The life story of a famous local could be written in the first person, or in diary form. You might even get away with a series of interviews with local ghosts. Instead of the author telling us who they were, how they died and why they haunt a particular place you could put it all into the first person. *A new approach to an old subject needs to be fresh, individual, quirky...*

Lots of books have been written about the Malvern Hills which divide Worcestershire from Herefordshire. The history has been explored, as have the links with Edward Elgar and other famous visitors or residents, plus ideas for walks and cycle rides over and around the hills, even the routes taken by aforementioned Elgar. It appeared that every aspect had been covered until, one day, I had an idea for something unusual. An end-to-end walk over the Hills, describing the views, the history, the people I met along the way, and adding the humour. My personal experiences file held a sufficient amount of information about the hills for me to make an immediate start and I had taken short walks on the hills and met strange folk, including a Druid, a lady exercising her llamas and a flasher. I could use them all. Then came the problem. If I was to undertake this walk what was I going to wear? Hiking boots and rucksack did not feature in my wardrobe but I did have a big handbag and my most sensible footwear was a pair of bright orange court shoes, which my husband pointed out would be very useful – when I broke my ankle they could be removed and waved in order to direct the air ambulance to where I was lying injured. His comments were added to my notes. And that's as far as it got because I never actually had the energy or the inclination to add the personal experience of that walk to my file. This happened several years ago and no one else, needless to say, has come up with my idea since. *A new approach to an old subject needs to be fresh, individual, quirky . . .*

TIPS

- ◆ **Define the area you want to cover**. It will be easier to write about one area of your town than it would to tackle the town in its entirety.
- ◆ **Don't include too much information**. Make sure you do not stray from your original plan. If you have then cut out the irrelevant information and put it to one side, ready for the next book.
- ◆ **Keep it local**. Some aspects of your book may not be unique to the area you are writing about so don't get into their entire history. e.g. Elgar has a connection to the Malvern Hills but there is no need to include a complete history of Elgar in your book about those hills.
- ◆ **Do not aim for an encyclopaedia-sized book**. Think about the pricing of it. Local interest books tend to be paperback and reasonably priced.
- ◆ **Consider illustrations and/or photographs**. Make sure they are attention grabbing and will appeal to anyone browsing through the available local history titles. Remember to get permission to use photos and illustrations if they do not belong to you. Do not breach copyright.

Collecting other people's personal experiences

This is a way of getting others to help you write your book. Search your Personal Experiences file for a subject you care about and then search out others who feel the same way or have contrasting opinions.

Philip M. Adams is a librarian. For his library's centenary he decided to talk to some of the local residents and produce a pamphlet. Each person he spoke to told him their personal experience of living in the St John's area of Worcester, and then passed him on to a friend or relative because they had a good story to tell. The pamphlet grew and grew as the personal experiences were committed to paper. The residents recalled what had happened to them during the war, their time in the old orphanage and their schooldays, how they had worked the land, become office staff or factory workers. They remembered long-gone streets and buildings, some told of their experiences of the wars. Memories stretched from the final years of the 1800s up until the 1970s. The pamphlet stretched to 480 pages, eventually becoming a heavy-weight book filled with enough material to keep the most prolific novelist in ideas for life. (*Memories of St John's*, edited and compiled by Philip M. Adams)

Philip's collection of stories are all linked by place – St John's on the West side of the River Severn in Worcester. Anyone could copy this idea or collect together lots of stories with the same theme. To make a venture like this a success you need to choose a theme close to your heart – something you have personal experience of or a personal interest in.

Choosing a subject close to your heart

If you were adopted you might want to interview others in the same situation and ask them how they found out, and if they felt the need to discover their birth parents. There are hundreds of questions to be asked and if one of your personal experiences is adoption then you will know what those questions are.

Do you belong to a self-help group? These groups abound and cover all sorts of problems and experiences. They range from Alcoholics Anonymous to Writing Groups. There are groups for parents who have lost a child, women who have undergone hysterectomies, young mothers who suffer from post-natal-depression, gamblers and bankrupts. If it's a problem then there will be someone out there coping with it and a group trying to help. Whatever the group, if enough individual members are willing to be interviewed then you could have yourself a book. And if you have personal experience of the subject, or a personal interest, then this will shine through your work because you won't be simply exploring an idea. You will feel personally involved.

Linking with anniversaries

There are always anniversaries on the horizon and if one happens to coincide with one of your personal experiences, hobbies or interests then you could interview people linked with the occasion and write up those interviews as a book. It is no use going back 100 years. Try 50 instead, or ten. It will be easier to find interviewees. If it is soon to be 50 years since the town's hospital opened, or closed, then talk to retired nurses and ex-patients. You only need one because that one will pass you on to someone else and they will suggest someone else... Just like Philip's your book will grown and grow.

Writing biographies

Sometimes we are so close to people that we take them for granted and lose sight of the fact that, to others, they might be fascinating. If you don't think your life's exciting enough to write about then you could write about someone else's. You may already know, know about, or be personally linked to someone who has a great story to tell. Whether they are alive or long-dead you could write their biography for them. All you need is enough personal interest in their life.

This person could be listed in your file of Personal Experiences. Remember the ten *interesting* people you listed? One or more of them might be begging to have their story put into words.

Your family tree might provide you with someone interesting to write about. Older family members can often fill in gaps for you. Their personal experiences can give you the feeling of attachment to the person you would need in order to do their life story justice. You need to care about whoever your subject is.

Tracy Baines, a freelance writer, recalls, 'My Grandmother would tell me about the men in the family who had been trawler skippers. She often talked of the hardships of life at sea and the struggle of the women left behind. One brother was skipper of a ship that was lost at sea with all hands off the Old Man of Hoy in the Orkneys. It was well documented – the family was well known in the Grimsby area and I had read old newspaper articles about the event. She said his death was the first real shock that happened to her and after that all the other disasters seemed to hurt a little less.' Using those facts, combined with knowledge passed on from her grandmother, Tracy wrote a piece that was published in the local paper. Over the years, she added to her files and discovered that she had enough information about the work of the Mission for Deep Sea Fishermen to write an article which she sold to *The Lady*. With two published pieces under her belt Tracy could be classed as an expert on the subject and, inspired by her grandmother's tales, she aims to write a novel about the fishing families of Grimsby.

Ghosting

Think back to the opening lines of this chapter. *It is said that everyone has a book in them. Yes. It is the story of their own life.* What should be added is that not everyone has the ability to write their life story. But they might like to pay you to do what they can't. Write it down.

Ghosts do exist. I've been one! I drew on my personal experiences in order to write about someone else's life as if it was my own. I knew what it was like to fall in love, to be short of money, to be pregnant... I could step inside the skin of the lady I was writing for – not on every occasion, but I was able to transfer my emotions to her life and to describe those emotions in ways that she was unable to.

Life stories can deal with all sorts of despair, depravation and depravity. There have been books about selling children into slavery, children who were locked away for years on end, abused, starved... Many stories are told by the victims because they have survived it all and emerged on the other side. Many are written by ghost writers and have become hugely successful. These are the dramatic stories which appear in the real life magazines but have enough material to make a book.

Before you leap into life as a ghost you should think carefully. Always listen to your client's story in full before deciding whether to take it on. You can do without any nasty surprises cropping up. (Three quarters of the way through the book I was working on my client calmly said, 'I suppose we should include the paedophilia'.)

You should also draw up a contract and be aware of the money side of things. How will you be paid? Who is responsible for forking out expenses? What happens if one of you suddenly decides they do not want to continue? Do not step into a ghost's shoes lightly!

INTERVIEWING TECHNIQUES

Don't go for the now fashionable approach, often seen on television, where the reporter shoves a microphone under the interviewee's nose and says, 'Tell us what happened' or worse still, 'Talk about yourself for a bit'.

In my capacity as a reporter for a local newspaper I interviewed plumbers, carpenters, builders and wine bar owners, to name a few. My editor did not realise how little my experience was when it came to interviewing. Let's be honest. I had no experience. Being a freelance writer had got me the job. No one knew that my only published work was a Reader's Letter. This was a case of being thrown in at the deep end, with no water-wings. Thankfully the business people I spoke to didn't know this. They were probably as frightened of me as I was of them. My learning curve was steep and swift.

One of my first lessons was to phrase questions carefully so that the answer could not be a simple yes or no. Monosyllabic answers do not help anyone to write up several hundred words. Next I learned to take note of the most interesting line I was given and use it as my opener. Hence the feature I wrote on the man who ran a roof insulation business began with, 'A house without loft insulation is like a teapot without a cosy'.

If you are going to commit someone's memories to tape then switch on your tape as you knock on the front door. Excited contributors to your book may well start recounting their stories as you are still wiping your feet on the mat. The sparkle from the first telling is often lost if you have to ask them to repeat their story.

In today's busy world there is not always time to interview face to face, especially if your subject lives many miles away. Telephone interviews can be awkward for the writer as these calls, due to new technology, can no longer be taped unless you have the right equipment. If you don't then you will need to make notes quickly, brush up on the short-hand, or have a good memory.

Email interviews are popular. You have plenty of time to decide on your questions and then email them to your subject. This is an easy method if you are interviewing another writer because their answers will be well written. Not so simple if your interviewee is the type who would need a ghost writer to tell his/her life story. You will have to word questions very carefully in order to get the answers you want and you may have to send several emails in order to clarify the answers you receive.

SIX TOP TIPS

◆ If possible, search out some information about the person before you interview them.

◆ Don't be late for your appointment/phone call.

◆ Never ask questions which can be answered with a yes or no.

◆ Don't interrupt or be tempted to tell them of your own personal experiences.

◆ LOOK and listen – it's not only the words that make the person.

◆ Always phone or write to thank the interviewee afterwards.

PART TWO

Fiction

7

What Is Fiction?

A DEFINITION

The dictionary defines fiction as *something invented by the imagination*. That's the definition of a lie too, isn't it? I have heard one writer describe his job as 'writing lies on bits of paper and selling them'.

In the same dictionary fiction is described as *an assumption of a possibility as a fact, irrespective of the question of its truth*. That means that we, as writers, assume that something that is actually possible, but that has not happened, is real.

EXAMPLE

An assumption of a possibility as a fact – I have not won millions on the lottery but it is a possibility that one day I might. A remote one maybe, but we can assume this as a possibility. It is not true to say that I have won millions on the lottery but now we have decided that there is a chance that this could happen then we can make it happen in fiction. We can assume that it is real, *irrespective of its truth*. And once we have done this we can write a fictional story wherein I have won the millions and am happily spending them on myself, my friends and family. That is fiction.

Comparing fiction with real life

Fiction is not real. It bears little relation to accounts of things that really happened. Yet fiction has to seem like real life, and your job as the writer is to persuade the reader that it is real life despite the fact that life is often boring, drags on and the unfolding of a real life story could take years or, as often happens, there is no satisfactory end to a problem.

In real life a loved one goes away alone on holiday, business or for any other reason and never returns. For years those who love him search for him. They wonder where he is, why or how he went missing, if he is still alive and, if so, what he is doing now. They spend their lives searching for him or for information about him, but eventually they die without ever knowing what happened. In fiction we could not write this story. It would need to be resolved. This man would need to be found and a satisfactory explanation given as to why he went missing in the first place and what he has been doing in the intervening space of time.

Fiction would tidy all of this up for us. We have a problem – man goes missing – and a satisfying ending – man is found – in a short space of time, or words. There can be no blow by blow account of proceedings – all those days, weeks or years of searching with no results – otherwise the reader would get bored, especially a child. We have to present them with an exciting, and satisfying, short form. Here it is – man goes missing, clue discovered soon afterwards, flashback to his life in order to find out why he would disappear, then a realisation of where he could be, and finally his discovery and a resolution of the problems which made him 'lose' himself in the first place.

Years ago a police inspector was interviewed on radio about the influx of new recruits since *The Bill* had become popular on television. 'The trouble is,' he said, 'that these young men and women expect all the crimes to be solved in 30 minutes as they are on television.' There is the difference between real life and good fiction.

TURNING FACT INTO FICTION

The best advice is not to let the truth get in the way of entertainment. You will have to learn to tell lies in order to change your story from real life to fiction. A few lies will always improve your story and telling lies isn't a bad thing to do if it helps to make your story interesting. You will need new techniques to turn your factual accounts into publishable fiction.

Embellishing, adding, exaggerating...

These are the things you need to do in order to turn a personal experience into a fictional story. Take your personal experience and change the real life characters into other people. Change the setting. Make the ending more exciting. The truth isn't always good enough and yet sometimes truth really is stranger than fiction. When that happens you, as a writer, have to work at your story or novel and make it sound convincing. That is what fictionalising it is all about.

EXAMPLE

At a writers' group Audrey read a story about her childhood. She was an elderly lady and wrote well. Her story told of the days before the NHS when Audrey needed an operation which the family couldn't afford to pay for. Her father collected together all of the family's possessions and pawned them but, still having only a portion of the funds needed, he took the lot to the racecourse and put every penny on a horse. Audrey's final paragraph was about how the horse won the race, her father arrived home triumphant and she went off to hospital for surgery. 'And every word is true,' finished Audrey proudly.

All of the writers listening agreed that this was an amazing story but it was too easy. We urged her to change the end. Most of the suggestions given involved the horse race. What about a close finish and Audrey's Dad having to wait to see which horse was declared the winner?

'But it was an outright winner,' said Audrey.

'How about a steward's enquiry?'

'There wasn't one,' said Audrey digging in her heels. She refused to change a word 'because that's the way it happened'. And that is fine but she was hoping to sell this story as fiction to a women's magazine.

No amount of persuasion would get her to change her mind. An improved version with embellishments added to give some suspense at the end was not for her. She was not going to distort the truth in order to entertain her readers. She could have sold this story as real life but she wanted to fictionalise it so that it became a short story, and yet she couldn't bring herself to tell any lies. And what are lies if not fiction?

Adding black moments

Audrey could have added a Black Moment to her story. This is when, just as everything seems to be working out well, the writer throws in a final problem. Think Indiana Jones here. He runs across a rope bridge to escape from a tribe of spear-throwing natives. They cut the ropes and we see him begin to plunge into the ravine but he manages to hang on as the bridge crashes against the cliff on the other side. He climbs painfully up the ropes. We see his hands grip safe ground at the top. His head lifts and ... no, he hasn't escaped! Another group of enemies stand waiting for him. That's a Black Moment. We all thought he'd made it and we were all fooled. It didn't end as we expected and the tale was a lot more exciting because of that.

Learn to lie

Audrey wasn't prepared to lie, exaggerate or embellish and therefore lost out on a good story. Do not do that. Do not stick to the truth, the whole truth and nothing but the truth. Remember that fiction is not truth. It only has to appear to be true. In other words it needs to sound believable. Learn to tell lies to improve your story.

My advice is – don't let the truth get in the way of entertainment. And if you can't do that then ask yourself the following question.

Should your story be fiction or non-fiction?

You could take any one of your personal experiences and turn it into fiction, or write it up as fact. Why, you need to ask yourself, should I fictionalise it?

- You want to improve it by telling a few lies, making a few alterations and/or additions.

- You have some unresolved problems and want to write yourself a happy ending.

- You want to protect the people who feature in your story.

- You do not want the general public to know that this is your real life story.

- You feel there is no market for it as factual writing.

More therapy

Fiction can be therapeutic too. If someone annoys you then murder them. Allow all that anger and frustration to pour out onto the page. My in-laws died many deaths. Killing them off always made me feel better, especially when they arrived for the weekend and stayed a fortnight.

Add a Murder Evening to your writing group's programme and listen to the members happily rid themselves of taxmen, sadistic teachers, corrupt MPs, noisy neighbours, scantily clad pop stars and, of course, partners. And in the most imaginative ways. It will prove so popular that it will have to became a regular event.

While the man in the street suffers we, as writers, can cheerily chop down our enemies and dispose of the bodies without any fear of the police knocking on our doors or of having to pay the price of our crime. If you are lucky a publisher may pay you. But beware. So many writers are murdering their spouses that some of the women's magazines now list it as a taboo subject. It's been done to death, you could say.

CONSTRUCTING CHARACTERS

Where can you get characters from if you don't use real people? A real flesh and blood person is a good starting point. How many people have you met during your lifetime? Any of them could become your characters. Refer back to your list of ten interesting people. All of them could feature in a story or novel. 'Oh, but they'd recognise themselves,' I hear some of you say. The answer is that they are most unlikely to.

Am I in it?

This is a question many writers are asked by friends and family who read their work. These readers fall into three categories.

◆ Type A: those who want to see themselves in print.

- Type B: those who are in print but don't recognise themselves.
- Type C: those who do recognise themselves because you haven't done your job properly.

Type A like to see themselves in every piece you write. They want to make an appearance. 'Is that me?' a friend will ask. 'Am I in it?' Auntie Elsie wants to know. My auntie's stairlift once featured in a story but my auntie certainly wasn't the rather nasty old woman who wouldn't let anyone touch her latest toy.

There is nothing that can be done about Type A, apart from trying to convince them that they do not make an appearance in your latest best-seller. If they are happy thinking they feature then why spoil it for them by telling them the truth?

Type B are actually in your work but don't recognise themselves because you have used an aspect of them that they do not see themselves. For instance, my father-in-law was the world's worst driver. He would complain that his car attracted sheep. 'Must be the colour,' he told me. 'They run at it.' He once drove through a pedestrianised area of town dodging not only oblivious shoppers but also large concrete bowls holding flowers. For the grand finale he bounced his poor car down three steps and back on to the road. This was a man I felt compelled to write about, and I did. Unfortunately he arrived when not expected and my story was sitting on the table. He picked it up, read it and exclaimed, 'He shouldn't be allowed on the road. What an idiot!'

You see, he had not recognised himself because, in his own eyes, he was a very good driver. It was all the others who were at fault. I had changed his appearance but not his personality traits as

seen by me. He simply didn't recognise those traits in himself.
Type B do not cause problems.

Type C are the people who do recognise themselves because you
have used them exactly as they are. You have not changed their
appearance, habits, temper or whatever it is that makes them
unique. Unlike Type B these people's sense of themselves is more
developed – they can see their own faults as well as their good
side. I once used a friend in a book exactly how he was but only
because he had died. Writing about him proved therapy for me
and I dedicated the book to his memory.

Type C are the problem ones so you need to reassure them that
they can't possibly be the murder victim or the murderer or
whoever else they see themselves as. Point out that the victim
bleached her hair blonde and when they tell you that is what they
do, pretend you always thought their hair colour was natural.
There are ways of wriggling out of the problem. 'Of course it isn't
you. You'd never do anything that nasty.' This situation should
never occur. There is an easy solution. Do not use friends
wholesale. Learn to pick and mix.

Pick and mix

Have you seen those books for children that have the pages cut
into three so there's a head on the top third, a body on the
second, and legs and feet on the bottom part? Each section can be
flipped over separately thereby making many different characters.
Making fictional characters is a bit like that and chopping up real
people can produce interesting results.

I once had a boss who frequently used to partake of liquid

lunches and then sing to us in the afternoon. 'Any requests?' he'd call from his office. He had got a good voice and he wasn't bad looking, but he was stuck in a time-warp and wore white suits with flared trousers and wide lapels long after they'd gone out of fashion. So far I've cut him into three. I gave his singing voice to one character, his drinking habits to another and his dress sense to yet another.

Another idea is to take a fat friend and make them thin, or vice-versa. I've used friends and family members as a basis for characters. I've taken the looks of one and the dress sense of another, then sprinkled into the mix the wit, kindness or maturity that I had seen in others. This recipe is guaranteed to give good results and it is easier to write about a 'fictional' character if you can see them in your mind's eye, hear the sound of their voice and know their traits inside out.

You could also try a sex change. This too can produce successful results. That awful woman at Writers' Circle, the one who has vinegar instead of blood and can never say anything nice about anyone or their work. Turn her into a man, give her a moustache (don't bother if she's already got one), give her her comeuppance in a story and read it out right under her nose. She won't ask, 'Am I in it?' because, like my father-in-law, she won't recognise herself. And this, once again, is wonderful therapy.

It can be great fun shopping for characters. You should never come home from the supermarket without one. Last week a giant of a young man was in front of me in the queue. The mountain of biscuits, cakes and frozen ready-meals in his trolley was threatening an avalanche. I don't know him, don't know his name or anything about him and he doesn't know me so I'll take him wholesale, exactly as seen. Two friends of mine, both novelists, had an argument one day when the three of us were having lunch together. It began over the waitress who had red Cupid's bow lips, blue-black hair and pointed breasts. 'I want her,' said Rob. 'No, she's mine,' said Dee. Me, I kept quiet and put her in a short story the very next day.

EXERCISE

Remember that list of ten *interesting* people you made? Now is the time to take another look at it. Give each one a page in your notebook and then begin listing their characteristics. These could include looks, dress sense, habits, personality, talents . . . Now swap these around so that Character 1 is no longer tall, thin and grey but short and plump with a comb-over which were the looks of Character 6. Give Character 1 the limp that Character 3 had. Make him happy and carefree like Character 9.

Eventually you will end up with a set of completely new characters. These people will appear real to your reader because, in your personal experience, all the separate bits of them are real.

Naming your characters

If it makes life easier for you, use real names for your characters – the names of those they most closely resemble. But make sure that once your work is complete you find and replace them. This is very easily done now we have computers.

My mother once gave me an idea for a story when she said she could do with getting married again, just for the presents. She didn't want the man. My first version of the story contained my mother, brothers and aunties. All names were changed in the final rewrite. This method made it easier for me to write, and it was fun.

Names go in and out of fashion. Years ago royal names were popular – Elizabeth, Margaret and Philip. Now children are more likely to be named after pop celebrities. Flower names have made a return in recent years. Choose your characters' names with care. They need to fit the age of the person you are writing about. If your character is five years old, or fifty, then consider who you know in that age group. What are their names and those of their contemporaries? There will probably be several to choose from.

Giving settings to characters

Characters need to be somewhere in order to play out their story. New writers sometimes forget this and have several paragraphs at the start where two or more characters are talking through their problems but do not appear to be anywhere. There is no mention of setting and, for all the reader knows, they could be floating about in the ether.

The main character, setting and problem should be as close to the beginning of your story or novel as possible in order for the reader to feel as if they are with someone in a specific place and beginning to feel sympathy for one of the characters.

Settings can be as ordinary as a kitchen, as glamorous as an exotic beach or celebrity party, or as imaginative as another planet. You can use the real thing or invent a new place, which you would have to do if your characters were on another planet.

Writers often have a favourite place in which they set their novels. Think Daphne du Maurier and Cornwall. You might have a favourite setting too. It is perfectly acceptable to use a setting which exists. On the other hand you, as the all powerful author, can invent new places. These could be entirely new towns or new streets in existing towns. Take your home town and place imaginary streets in it, or even whole areas. Mix the town you live in now with the one hundreds of miles away that you grew up in, or spent holidays in. What you need to do is make your setting come alive for your reader. They have to be able to see it as they read. Using your personal experience of a place can do exactly that, and even if you make huge differences by adding new estates to a town or a new town to a county, if you have used real places then the reality should show through the writing. It's another case for Pick and Mix.

EXERCISE

Now is the time to go back to the list of ten *interesting* places you made. You could take any one of those and use it exactly as it is as a setting for a story but for this exercise you can play Pick and Mix again.

Mix several places to make one. Now take one place as you know it and add something extra to it – a new street, a house, an extra door, a statue. That something new might become the seed of a story. Once you have done this exercise ask yourself if you felt more comfortable with the settings as they actually exist or did you enjoy being an all-powerful architect?

PLOTTING

Many writers turn to their personal experiences in search of plots. You should already have some in your Personal Experiences file.

What about those ten *happy* occasions in your life, and those ten *sad* times? What about your job experiences? The items in your memory box, or the story behind a photograph? However large or small an experience was it can be turned into a story or become the starting point for a book.

Asking what if?

By repeatedly asking *what if?* you can arrive at a plot.

This morning the council arrived to collect and dispose of a mattress, but what if they hadn't turned up? I might have been the sort who would take it for a ride in the car late at night and dump it in a beauty spot. What if I had witnessed a murder while I was out there? Or, what if I had decided to burn it instead? What if the fire got out of control? What if flames leaped to the roof of the house? What if the roof caught fire? What if I kept a secret in the loft?

Writers should always be asking themselves what if? That's how they come up with plot ideas. It's also the reason for a percentage of them being unable to sleep at night. What if I wake up tomorrow and am the only person remaining in the world? What if I lose my memory during the night? What if I wake up in a strange room? All those *what ifs?* are possible scenarios, possible problems, possible solutions.

Exploring parallel universes

Writing fiction is like exploring parallel universes. There is a theory that there are an infinite number of parallel universes to our own, and in each there is another version of us. In this one you are reading this book, in another you have put it down to watch television, in yet another you didn't bother buying it. (Let's not go there.)

Think about it. In a parallel universe you didn't marry the partner you have here. You are with someone else. You have had six partners. You are single. In a parallel universe your bank balance has lots more zeros on the end balance. In a parallel universe you are a famous writer.

This theory will allow you to come up with an infinite number of stories. Try applying it to all sorts of situations, relationships and problems in your Personal Experiences file, and you get a story. Even better, each story has an infinite number of possibilities. Take this opening line:

Glenda opened the envelope, read the contents and sat for a moment, stroking the thick paper.

Now apply the law of parallel universes to it and you could have:

Glenda didn't open the envelope.

Glenda opened the envelope but was unable to read the contents.

Take it further and Glenda could have been standing up or lying down when she opened or didn't open the envelope. The envelope could have been a parcel. The moment could have been ten minutes, fifteen, an hour. . .

Instead of stroking she could have ripped, set fire, flushed away. . . the thick paper, thin paper, blue, pink, scented paper. . . Perhaps there was no paper. Perhaps there was something else in the envelope. There are an infinite number of 'something elses'. And

Glenda can be called by any other name. Glenda need not be a she. It could be all be happening to Bill. Every variation leads to a new plot.

Achieving the dreaded 'show, don't tell'

You either grasp this concept or struggle with it. The first part of this book is about using personal experiences to write non-fiction. Non-fiction is all about telling, or informing, the reader of facts or events. Imagination needs to be kept out of it. The headline in a newspaper is 'Baby Snatched'. The story begins:

A woman in the city centre snatched a baby from its buggy on Monday afternoon. Jodie Jones, aged 31, grabbed the one year old from his mother, Simone Smith.

That is telling. It gives the facts and nothing else. A novice writer who hasn't grasped the theory of 'show, don't tell' might expand it to something like this:

Jodie waited until the woman wasn't looking, then she ran across the precinct and snatched the baby from its buggy.

To show this story you need to see it happen, feel what the people involved are feeling, and when expanded give motives for what happened.

Jodie was amazed to see how violently her hands were shaking. She tried to swallow but her mouth was dry. She knew what she was about to do was wrong. The baby belonged to Simone. 'But he's also Darren's,' she told herself. And Darren wanted him back.

She waited inside the shop door. Finally Simone turned away from her child. Her hand was still on the buggy but her eyes were on the new man in her life – the one who had crept up behind to surprise her. Now it was Jodie's turn to creep. Quickly, soundlessly she crossed the precinct. Her hands reached out towards the little boy. His body felt warm and firm. His tiny hands clutched at hers as she clicked his safety straps open and lifted him...

When I was working for the newspaper my fictional stories became flat and boring. It took me a while to work out the reason why. It was because they were being told as in reporting, and not shown as in writing fiction. It can take time to change from one kind of writing to another. It's all writing but there are different forms, just as in running there are sprints and marathons. Both are running but they have completely separate techniques.

CONVEYING EMOTIONS

Getting inside the skin

In order to show what is happening in a story you need to be inside your character's skin. Jodie is feeling fear. You need to sift through your personal experiences to discover a time when you were frightened or extremely nervous. Look in your file at those incidents that scared you. Draw on one, or several, of those incidents to relive those feelings – and then write them into the scene you are working on.

Try writing the scene in the first person. It may help to live it through yourself and it can be changed into the third person later.

Teresa Ashby, one of the most prolific and well known short story writers, explains how, by using personal experience, you can get inside the skin of a character who is anxious.

> *'Your main character is an anxious mother watching her not-very-confident four year old walk into school for the first time. You don't have kids? Don't know how that feels? Yes you do. We've all loved someone or something and had to leave them at some point to face a worrying unknown.*

> *'How about that time your dog had to be left at the vet's for an operation and the last you saw of her was her miserable, frightened little face peering at you before the nurse closed the door?*

> *'Don't have a dog? Well okay, that story you put everything into and posted an hour ago? What if some kid with a match and a twisted sense of humour decides to have some fun? What if the editor spills her coffee all over it?*

> *'Anxiety is just one emotion, but you know how it feels so write about it.*

> *'Write about how you feel about the child but think about the dog or the story or whatever else you have been anxious about. That's your personal experience. It's all in the feeling, something we all have and the beauty of it is that it's transferable.'*

Glynis Scrivens, a writer based in Australia, writes for both the Australian and British women's magazine short story markets. She confirms what Teresa says but also advises against using emotions which are still fresh and raw.

'It's where I try to use things that affect me deeply that I either strike gold or come unstuck. That seems to be the nature of the beast. It all depends how much space I can put between me and . the event. What works best is if I write the story when the pain/ embarrassment/whatever emotion is fresh, then let it sit on the backburner. It's only after I've talked things over with a friend, and the situation is resolved, that I can see how to shape what I've written.

'One ploy I've only recently learnt is to use just the emotion of an experience and translate it to a completely new scenario. So if I've had an argument with my daughter which has upset me, for example, I might write a scene where a woman has an argument with her husband.'

EXERCISE

Take some time to explore your emotions. Think back through your personal experiences, dig deeply into your emotions and write about:

◆ A time when you felt elated.
◆ An event which caused you anxiety.
◆ A time when you felt joy.
◆ That occasion when you felt fear.
◆ A situation that made you angry.
◆ How it feels to be frustrated.

EXERCISE

Using the emotion most closely involved in your personal experience, write about the following:

◆ A birth.
◆ A marriage.
◆ A death.

Now tip them on their head and try again. For instance, sorrow and grief are usually associated with death. But what if a death caused one of your characters joy? Try the transference method that both Teresa and Glynis use and see how it works for you.

Exploring your emotions in fiction can be difficult. If you have shared the anger or sorrow felt by a character in a book, take another look at those particular passages and analyse how the author has managed to instil these emotions into you. He or she will be drawing on their own experiences in order to arouse your emotions.

Think back to your own life and its ups and downs when you want to explore emotions. Use that painful memory to write pain, explore that moment of sheer joy to write joy.

Make 'em laugh, make 'em cry

One writer's short stories that are guaranteed to bring a tear to the eye are those of Irene Yates. I asked her the secret of writing emotional stories.

> *'For the writer, there are always two emotions to be considered,'*
> *she says. 'Character emotion and reader emotion. While I'm*
> *writing something, in my head, always, is the idea of the emotion*

I want to produce in my reader. Usually I want to make them laugh or make them cry. Often I want them to do both. When I have written, I know that if the story doesn't do what I want it to do, for me, it won't do it for my reader. If it stops my heart, then it will stop the reader's heart.

'To make sure that it does, I work and work and work on the words. I know the meaning of what I want to say but I work on saying it in the most effective way possible. This means that I can work on one sentence many, many times to get it to produce the emotion I really want. There is a world of difference between "Jane felt scared" and "Something tightened in Jane's throat, choking off her breath". Likewise, your character can cry or her eyes can fill up with tears. She can feel angry or her green eyes can smoulder with sudden fire. My best friend is my thesaurus!'

EXERCISE

Write a paragraph (or more) about the following:

◆ Being with a person or animal as they died.
◆ Your first kiss.
◆ Holding your child or grandchild for the first time.
◆ That time when you lost your temper and felt capable of murder.

The splinter of ice

Writers tend to stand on the sidelines and watch life passing by. They feed off everything that happens either to themselves or to those around them. Have you ever watched the reactions of someone who is undergoing some trauma and stored it to use in your writing? Does writing about a personal or dramatic incident and the emotions attached to it make you feel guilty, especially if they are another's experiences and not your own? Have you ever found yourself watching something awful and thinking I can use that? A road accident, for example. Someone suffering? A grieving widow at a funeral or a couple standing over an injured child. Lots of terrible situations crop up in life. We may be directly involved or find ourselves as the onlooker.

EXAMPLE

It's happened to me. I was alone, driving along narrow twisting lanes over the top of a mountain. There wasn't a light in sight. It was 2 a.m. and added to the darkness was a thick mist. Suddenly a white shape shambled across the road in front of the car. It glowed in the headlights. A soggy Welsh sheep.

This is a perfect setting for a spine-chiller, I thought and then cursed myself for being heartless. An emergency call from the hospital was the reason for my journey. 'He's taken a turn for the worse. We think you should be here,' the nurse had told me on the phone. My husband was sick, really sick, and all I could think about was a setting for a story. I couldn't possibly be human!

Things got worse. I don't mean the patient. He made a great recovery. I mean me. Patients in the other beds were so interesting. So were their visitors. Instead of talking to my husband I found myself jotting down thoughts, feelings, characters, bits of dialogue. Several pages of a notebook were filled as I sat alongside his hospital bed.

I hated myself for being able to do that – think about writing while my world was maybe coming to an end.

'I'm not human,' I confessed to Janie Jackson.

'RememberThe Snow Queen?' she asked. 'The little boy, Kay, who had the splinter of ice in his heart? Writers can be like that. There's a part of us that can stand to one side and do the observing bit, even while dreadful or emotional events are taking place.'

Graham Greene called it 'the splinter of ice in the heart of a writer.'

It's not the easiest bit of being a writer to come to terms with. At least I know I am not alone and am beginning to accept it as part and parcel of being a writer. So, don't feel guilty if you come across your own ice splinter.

STRENGTHENING YOUR WRITING

Using the five senses

By using the five senses you can strengthen your writing. Don't go overboard and add all five to one scene. One or two will be sufficient.

Sight

This covers description of character, setting scenery, dress, food... You can describe anything or anyone in your story or novel thus allowing them to be 'seen' by the reader.

EXERCISE

Look up from this page. Pick up your exercise book and pen, then focus on one or two aspects of wherever you are sitting, be it in the house or garden, on a bus or train. Now write a description of your surroundings. Write what you see.

Taste

Considering there are only four basic flavours, writers have found endless ways of describing them. Sweet, salt, sour and bitter are the flavours our taste buds detect. Food is not judged on taste alone so other senses will come into play when describing food. Appearance (sight) is important if you want to tempt a jaded appetite. Texture plays an important part too. If everything on your plate is pureed where's the interest?

EXERCISE

Experiment with a food from each category. Look at it, touch it, taste it. Then describe it.

Smell

Smell and taste are closely related. Strongly scented foodstuffs, like bacon or kippers, can make you feel as if you are tasting them. Smells can be good, bad, tempting. They can lure you towards them or drive you away. They can make your mouth water or make you want to vomit. Kitchens smelling of warm bread and freshly brewed coffee are pleasant places, as well as being an estate agent's dream. Cellars that are dank, fusty and musty are not.

EXERCISE

Go and sniff a few items, pleasant and unpleasant and then return to your notebook and try to write a few descriptive words about each.

Sound

Complete silence is rare. There is always a sound close by. Writers need to listen in to background sounds. Their characters might be half asleep but what is happening around them? There could be a tap dripping, preventing sleep, or a child crying. Does the sound fill the void of the night? Is it gentle, piercing, soft? Sound can affect the ears and the teeth. Think of chalk scraping on the blackboard. Sound can also vibrate through the body. At this moment I can hear the clock ticking, the computer humming and a fly has just flown into the window. It made the tiniest tap as it came into contact with the glass.

EXERCISE

Listen. What do you hear? Listen carefully to every sound. Concentrate on one at a time. Shut your eyes and do it NOW. Then write down descriptions of those sounds.

Touch

Writing should include texture, the feel of things. The softness of a blanket, the warmth of a bed, a cold night can all be expanded upon. How cold was the night? How soft the blanket? You want your reader to feel what your character is touching. You also want them to join in the sensations they are experiencing. Note how your body reacts to extremes of hot and cold. What does comfort feel like? How do you describe pain?

EXERCISE

Put your index finger in this page so as not to lose your place. Now close the book over it. Try to put into words what it feels like to have your finger crushed gently between the pages. Slide your thumb over the cover. What does that feel like? Is the texture smooth and shiny? How smooth? How shiny? Does your thumb slide easily or stick to the cover?

Think back to the last time you were in pain. The last time you were totally relaxed. The last time your fingers and toes were numb from cold. Describe each. Write it all down in your file.

Being specific

Another ploy to strengthen writing is to be specific. If your character gets into his car there is no picture. By being specific and naming the type of car, describing it as red and sleek, you are not only giving a picture of the car but also adding to the readers' knowledge of your character. A battered Mini or a shining Rolls Royce will not be driven by the same type of person.

Take an item of clothing such as a hat and make it specific. A woolly hat can conjure up many images, none of them specific. Make it knitted in stripes of black and yellow, like a bumble bee and your reader has a specific picture.

Or if you have Lynsey stopping on her way to slimming club to peer in at the window of the baker's shop make sure your reader sees the temptations. Don't say cakes. Be specific. Make them over-large vanilla slices, glossy with white icing, the yellow custard threatening to burst from the layers of flaky pastry. Think in pictures. Imagine someone having to create an illustration for each paragraph of your story. Would they be racking their brains or would they have that array of pastries to paint?

8

Short Stories

KNOWING THE MARKETS

There are three basic markets for short stories. Magazines, small press and competitions. A well established novelist, one who is a household name, might warrant an anthology of their short stories. Otherwise a collection of stories by one writer is rare, unless self-published.

Competitions are run by writing groups, magazines, town councils and organisations. News of these can be found on writers' websites, in libraries, newspapers and magazines. There are also newsletters, such as *Freelance Market News*, which are filled with not only news of competitions but all sorts of opportunities for writers. Small press magazines, such as *The Yellow Room*, take stories. Most of these are run on shoe-string budgets and cannot afford to pay, or pay very little, but many are well respected and a story in them will look good on your CV.

The largest and most popular market for stories is the women's magazine market. Magazines constantly change. They take stories, then they don't. They want certain lengths, certain genres. You may hear that the market is dwindling but do not focus on the number that have stopped using fiction, concentrate instead on the number that are producing more issues, more specials, all containing short fiction.

USING YOUR PERSONAL EXPERIENCES

You will be able to put your personal experiences to full use regardless of the market you are writing for. It is the added personal experience that can make a story sound authentic and give it that touch of magic – the sparkle every writer needs. It is impossible to keep you out of your stories. This is because we only know what is in our own experience, whether we have lived it, know someone else who has, or we've seen it on the television, heard it on the radio or the news, read it in books or newspapers. Because it is impossible to keep personal experience out of your work, why not revel in it? Enjoy it.

Many times, when I've mentioned writing short fiction for women's magazines, the reaction is, 'Oh, they're all love stories'. The content of magazine short stories is very varied and girl-meets-boy is not what they are all about. Today's stories are about what happens to us, our family members, our friends, the girl on the supermarket check-out, the hairdresser. The problems involved are those that can concern any of us – demanding babies, rebellious teenagers, buying houses, juggling too many demands, understanding the needs of elderly relatives, coping and coming to terms with the death of a loved one. They are about relationships.

Tell the world about it

Writers of short fiction tend to explore what is going on in their own life at that particular time. Their children are starting school. They think they are suffering from empty-nest syndrome, somewhere amongst their acquaintances the break-up of a relationship is going on, or a wedding, a funeral. They are about to become a grandmother. It's all grist to the mill, all personal experiences to be added to their file and used then or later.

Stranger than fiction

Truth can be stranger than fiction so there are a few of your experiences which may be too unbelievable or coincidental to make fiction. It is no use telling an editor that 'this really happened to me' if they say your plot is too contrived.

Joan went halfway around the world to visit New Zealand and on one of the beaches met a man she had not seen for 40 years. She considered turning this into a happy-ever-after story, with him being her first love and then the two of them reconnecting after four decades. In the end she didn't use the story of their actual meeting. In real life it was one of those amazing coincidences but in fiction it would have sounded too manufactured.

All my stories have something of me in them. When a family member's ashes were thrown off the pier I wrote about it. When I helped my mother to move into a flat the experience provided enough material for three stories. When I was given roller-boots as a birthday present, the time I was on the village hall committee, when what I thought was a field mouse grew to huge proportions and visited a kitchen cupboard, when a town friend came to visit us deep in the countryside – they all provided stories for me.

My memory aids have provided me with ideas. My collection of pottery pigs became a story as did a photograph of me dressed as a chicken for a school fete, an entry from a school diary and a letter from a pen-friend.

I use everything that crops up in my life. I told readers about my move to the country, my problem with claustrophobia, how my father-in-law crashed his car, about my husband's heart attack. Nothing is sacred and now, as they enter the door, visitors are warned with the words, 'Be careful what you say. It could be taken down and used in a story.'

Pick up any women's magazine and it's a safe bet that Della Galton's name will be in it. Della says:

> '*I regularly use personal experience in my stories – it has to come from somewhere! Even if it's as little as just using the names of people I've recently spoken to, as character names. But more often than not my stories are sparked off by something someone has said to me – particularly if it's moving or touching in some way. Saying that, I don't breach confidentiality, and it has to be done sensitively, which is the advice I'd give to other writers too. Otherwise you might quickly end up with no friends!'*

Paula Williams's first published story, *Angels on Oil Drums*, was based on an incident from childhood when she bullied her five-year-old twin brothers into appearing in a play she'd written. Dressed as angels she made them stand on oil drums either side of the stage. When her eldest son was four he hated the big black cape she wore all through pregnancy. This was partly because she seemed to have no control over the swirling hem which used to clear shelves every time they went shopping, but also because one of his little friends used to call her Batman. This became the starting point for a story called *Here Comes Batman!*

> '*When you're a writer,' says Paula, 'no experience is ever wasted – not even the bad ones. When my brother fell through a roof and was in hospital for a long time I spent many anxious hours hanging about the hospital, particularly the restaurant. I got ideas, based on that setting, for three different stories and also*

found writing to be the best form of coping mechanism. It really helped to escape into a fictional world over which, because it was my creation, I actually had some control. And, on a happy note, my brother made a full recovery – and I sold all three stories.'

Short story writer, Elizabeth Moulder (Betty) says,

'I think I only write from personal experience. I probably lack imagination but do have an ear for the telling phrase. If I hear a quirky remark it registers and comes out later when I need it (thank goodness). An elderly neighbour, complaining that the advent of the telephone meant that you never got an unexpected visitor, gave me The Knock at the Door – *a story about a pensioner getting involved in disposing of the loot from a bank heist because some-one knocked on the wrong door and she was so bored she went along with the whole caper.* A Talent for Marriage *arose when a friend of mine embarked on a second (happy) marriage. She confided that her new husband was a bit of a hoarder and at the last count had 17 lawn mowers. My story was her clever solution.'*

Betty and I have been known to swap ideas, usually because they are too close to home and we feel we can't write them. Seek out other writers. We all need moral support, and writing friends may have stories they feel they cannot possibly use – specific incidents involving their children or parents, close friends or neighbours. You can swap story ideas with them. I always say every writer needs a Betty!

BORROWING PERSONAL EXPERIENCES

Your Personal Experiences file should be filling up by now, giving you plenty of ideas to explore in your writing. That does not mean you cannot use other people's experiences too. Why waste good material? A tall and well built friend, one of those capable, can cope with anything types, once confided in me that she would love to be small and fragile for a day and have someone take care of her instead of it always being the other way around. I couldn't wave a wand and reduce her in stature but I did write a story about her meeting someone taller and even more capable than she was who wanted to protect and care for her.

Friends share their problems, joys and successes. Add them to your file. You probably know someone who has been living with the same problem for years. They almost enjoy complaining about it. They ask for advice each time you meet up, and you know what they should do and possibly spend hours repeating the same advice, but do they listen? No. It's frustrating, isn't it? But don't let it raise your blood pressure. Go and solve their problem for them. Do it in writing. Change their name, their sex, their age. Set it all in a different context. For instance, if it concerns the ex-husband who won't let go turn him into a close friend who follows your every step. Write it and sell it. Your own personal experiences will be in there because a writer cannot help but include a few of their own opinions, some of their strengths or weaknesses.

Borrowing the bigger bits

If you are lucky you may be given an entire plot. All you need to do is add the characters, the setting and the sparkle. For instance when my mother signed up at the local college for lip-reading classes she would tell me about everything that had happened there each week. I soon had enough for a story. Add to that my knowledge of deafness – I'd been deaf for a few days after a severe cold, and I had experience of Mum's deafness and the problems it caused. That was all that was needed. Mum had several decades knocked off her age, her classmates were all dreamed up – especially the man she was going to end up with – the incidents she'd related were sprinkled in, and there it was, ready to sell. And it sold quickly because the subject matter was unusual.

Cultivate anyone you know who takes up an unusual sport or hobby, or signs up for an out of the ordinary class. Listen to them. Their personal experience could provide you with an entire story.

Choosing characters' ages

If your work is being written for a competition then the age of your characters probably will not be a factor, unless ages are stated in the requirements. However, if you are writing for a magazine you must think about the target age group it is aimed at. If you are 50 and write about a personal experience concerning that age then it won't sell to a magazine targeting the 21–35 year olds' market. I almost made this mistake when writing about the first time I ever looked after my grandson for a whole night. This was a twist-end story (see the end of this chapter for information about Twist Ends) in which the twist was the age of the character spending the night. I led the reader to believe the main character was talking about the new man in her life when it was actually her grandson. My printed pages were almost in the envelope when realisation dawned. The magazine I was sending my offering to did not use material about grandmothers. For a split second the thought that I had wasted my time crossed my mind and then another realisation dawned. The main character need not be a grandmother. She could shed those years at the touch of a few keys on the computer, drop a generation and become an auntie. Ten minutes later the new, younger, version was in that envelope. A few months after that the story appeared as *An Early Night*.

TINY PERSONAL EXPERIENCES

Little bits of personal experience, whether yours or borrowed, can provide the sparkle in a story. A long time ago Mary told me how she had been invited to a posh lunch. On arrival she was given a glass of sherry and there was wine with each course. She was feeling decidedly tipsy before the main course arrived and she was enjoying the company of a very nice man who was sitting next to her. He commented on her lovely brooch and how realistic it was. Mary couldn't remember putting on a brooch and looking down to check was dismayed to see a prawn, that had once adorned the salmon mousse starter, reclining on her chest. I knew I would use this one day. It didn't provide the storyline but it made a comical touch when I came up with a dinner party plot.

You do not need to use major crises in order to write a story. One tiny event can be enough as Jean Currie proved. The spark for her story may have been tiny, but it was also very annoying and gave Jean the impetus to write her own story with the end she wanted.

'It was not a normal fly. Normal flies buzz around for a bit, check out what they can find for lunch and run up and down the window trying to find a way out. Not this one. It buzzed round me non-stop. I shut it into the kitchen and sat down in the living room and there it was flying round my head. I left it in there, closed the door and sought refuge in my study. It followed. When I went to bed I couldn't sleep for the wretched thing round my head. It even followed me when I sought privacy in the bathroom.

There was only one answer. I should have to go out of doors. I took a chair into the shade of an oak tree and scribbled. All the fury and frustration poured from my pen. The woman in my story, pestered as I had been, eventually killed her tormentor. I don't know what happened to 'my' fly. I didn't see it again but I forgave it because I was paid for the story.'

Make dreams come true

If you encounter a problem, no matter how small, you could write about it and, like Jean, write your own happy end. (Happy for Jean, not the fly.) When writing fiction we have the opportunity to play god. We can take a real life problem and solve it in a story. We can direct friends' and family's lives in the direction we would prefer them to go. Writers have the power to give a friend the perfect partner or the job they want. Take a failing relationship and breathe new life into it. Allow someone who needs the money to have a lottery win or a sick person to regain health. Jean killed her pesky fly. I got rid of relations who had overstayed their welcome, and a monster who had moved into my grandson's bedroom. You too can be all powerful and put the world to rights. The possibilities are endless.

USING WHAT IF?

What if you take a memory from your Personal Experiences file and turn it into fiction? Listed in my file is a long list of jobs I have had. One of them was working as a box-office assistant in a theatre. Our town had a local drama group who would put on performances there, including pantomimes. One night a pretty, but shy, girl approached me to ask where the drama group were rehearsing. I began to wonder why she wanted to join. What if it was because she fancied one of the boys in the group? What if she hoped they would get to play the leading parts together? What if she wanted to be Cinderella to his Prince Charming? What if they were both hopeless at acting? My pretty and shy girl had joined the group to be close to this boy so how was this going to be achieved? What if they got minor parts in the forthcoming pantomime? What was her incentive in joining the group? To be close to him. What if...? And I had the solution. They were asked to play the two halves of the pantomime horse. You can't get any closer than that, can you?

By asking *What if?* Glynis Scrivens turned a real life event into a ghost story. She explains:

'A few years ago, on holiday at the beach, my husband, Den, and daughter, Amy, rescued a local fisherman who'd fallen down a cliff and ended up wedged halfway, saved by a sapling. Den had to stay and hold him, and keep him talking. Amy climbed back up the cliff to get help. She had to interrupt two gay lovers to ask if she could borrow a cell phone to call the ambulance.

'The sea rescue helicopter arrived, with police and ambulance. Den helped to strap the fisherman onto the stretcher and carry him to the top of the cliff. When he staggered over the last rock, hoping to rest on the grass and get his breath back, he met cameras and reporters and had a microphone thrust into his face.

'It was a dramatic segment on the television news that night. The whole story got told and retold dozens of times. Everyone got goose bumps.

'*Next day on the beach Amy found the fisherman's old towelling cap with his name written inside. More goose bumps. Imagine how we'd have felt if he'd been dead and we'd found his cap? How could I use this in a story?*

'*Exactly a year later, back at the beach and suffering from flu, I sat at the top of the cliff, with my notebook and pen. Maybe being sick helped. I couldn't remember all the details, just the bits that made an impression on me – the old cap, that strategic sapling, the injured man talking then passing out.*

'*I tried to re-invent the whole scene. And then I thought* what if he'd died? What if it was murder? What if his ghost re-enacted the fall a year later – today – to seek justice? *And that was my story. I had to change Amy into a dog, turn Den into a policewoman, lose the gay lovers, and kill off the fisherman.*'

ANECDOTES AREN'T STORIES

What happened to Glynis and her family that day provided an anecdote. On its own it was not a story. She added the extras to turn it into one. An anecdote is an incident. You tell it your friends to entertain them. Their reaction is good. They laugh, cry or are horrified, whichever you had hoped them to be. Then they tell you it should become one of your stories and you are seduced into thinking that your anecdote will be enough. It's amusing, exciting or entertaining – it made your friends laugh – therefore it will charm an editor, and it will sell. No. An anecdote is only the basis for a story. It will need to have a beginning and an end added.

Here's an anecdote

My grandson was frightened to go to sleep because, he said, there was a monster in his bedroom. My daughter and son-in-law weren't getting any sleep because of Dan and his monster. I suggested Dan's dad went upstairs with a big stick and a large box. 'Make a lot of noise,' I told him. 'Pretend you are chasing the monster and you catch it and put it in the box and then in the car and drive off with it. Go and have a pint and when you get home tell Dan you've dropped the monster off at the tip and it won't be able to find its way back.' So that's what he did, and it worked.

If it had been written up exactly as it happened it would have been amusing but to turn it into a fully formed story it needed more. It needed a beginning and an end. The catching of the monster would become only part of the story.

Adding a beginning

Stories begin with a character and a problem. My daughter became a single mother who was drooping from exhaustion because her son was keeping her awake every night and she couldn't cope with the invisible, and non-existent, monster that he believed was in his bedroom. Then another problem was added. The story began with her cooking a special meal as her boyfriend was going to come around and she had planned a romantic meal for two. She loved this boyfriend but wanted to be certain that her son would love him too. His real father hadn't taken any interest in the boy.

Now bring on the anecdote

Boyfriend arrives. Food is about to be dished up. Screaming

starts. The romantic meal is ruined because of the little boy's fears. No amount of persuading will get him back to bed. Then the boyfriend leaps into action. He fetches (you guessed it) a stick and large box from the garden shed, captures the monster and drives it away.

And the end

The son sees his mother's new boyfriend as a hero. The mother realises that the two have bonded. The reader sees that the boyfriend will make the perfect husband and father, gives a sigh and is satisfied that everything has worked out well.

The Monster Upstairs was inspired by a child who was frightened of going to bed. Then the 'what ifs?' were asked, the embellishments added together with the beginning and the end, and finally the story was sold in the UK and Australia.

WRITING TWIST ENDS

This type of story remains ever popular – a twist in the tail, or tale, as some magazines describe them. The 'twist' stories are not about lying to the reader. The author's task is to give a certain piece of information which will make the reader jump to the wrong conclusion. From there onwards the job of the author is to keep *misleading* the reader right up until the final line, when all is revealed.

Throughout life, and in all sorts of circumstances, we jump to conclusions and this is what the writers of twist-end stories have to make their readers do. The twists often involve the reader assuming they know the age or sex of the main character because of something that has been stated in the opening paragraph.

Linda Povey says she has seen, and written, stories where the reader believes the protagonist is a woman, but turns out to be a man, but rarely the other way round. In *Wired Up* an electrician is talking about the problems with rewiring houses and how unreasonable householders can be about the necessary disruption. The reader will think that an electrician is a man. They usually are, but not always. The twist in Linda's story is that the electrician is a she, not a he, and ends up with the man of the house.

One of my stories began with a personal experience and a *what if?* moment. In it a young woman is being warned by a friend not to place her advertisement. 'It could be dangerous,' she said. 'Don't let any of the men come to your house and don't go to theirs.' All the way through, without lying, I led the reader to believe that the woman was a prostitute. That's the conclusion I wanted them to jump to. In order to do that I let the reader see my main character meeting men in cafes, chatting to them, arranging to meet them later. Money changed hands. All the woman was really doing was writing speeches, usually for whoever was going to be the best man at a wedding. This truth was not told until the very last line.

My personal experience was of a man – a stranger – phoning me to ask if I would write a speech for him as he was going to be best man at a wedding. A friend had given him my number. He asked if he should come to my house or if I would go to his. Eventually we arranged to meet in a cafe in the city centre – somewhere 'safe'. I interviewed him, got enough information to write the speech, and met him again in the same place a week later to hand it over. We sat in the window seat and I watched people walk by, several of whom I knew, while my 'client' read through what I had written. He was happy with it, and began counting cash into my hands. Cue the *what if?* moment. What if passers-by saw a man handing over money to a young and beautiful woman? (Not me, you understand. I was already well into fictionalising events by this time.) I called my story *Services Rendered*. It was published under that title. It says it all, doesn't it?

That's how you can come across ideas for twist-endings. I did not lie to the reader. I simply withheld one fact – the woman in the story was writing speeches. Everything else was the truth but I was deliberately misleading the reader throughout into thinking this was prostitution.

When the reader gets to the end where the truth is finally revealed they should kick themselves. 'Why didn't I guess that? It's obvious.' They might even re-read the story to see where the writer has littered all the clues. We've all had embarrassing moments, perhaps got 'the wrong end of the stick'. These can be turned into twist-end stories. That wrong assumption provides the twist for the story, so writing it can be a case of starting at the end and working back to the beginning.

EXERCISE

Have you had any embarrassing moments when you leapt to the wrong conclusion? List any and see if they would be suitable to use as twist-ends.

EXAMPLE

Linda Povey got an idea for a twist at a writers' conference:

'A group of us were visiting a nearby town when a total stranger said to one of the party, "Hello there, John." The said John was bemused by this, until he realised he was still wearing his name badge.

'Later, I was talking to someone who'd recently been stuck in a lift. The story was particularly horrifying to me, as I have a morbid fear of enclosed spaces, including lifts. I got to thinking what would be worse than being stuck alone in a lift ...? The result was *Trapped*. I used the name badge experience for the twist. Young Susie is trapped in a lift with a middle-aged lecher. She deflects his unwanted attentions by pretending she is his daughter, whose mother he abandoned while she was pregnant with her. She achieves this by giving the name of the supposed father – which is his and an unusual one. But of course she is simply reading it from the name badge he has forgotten to remove from a conference he's been attending.'

A borrowed experience (John and his name badge) together with a personal fear and Linda came up with a story.

9

Novels

A NEW EXPERIENCE?

A novel sounds like hard work. The length is putting you off. You don't think you have anything to write about. You are not clever enough to write one. But a novel need not be hard work. It can be a joy to write. The number of words grow each day. Everyone has a subject in their Personal Experiences file which could make a novel and, of course, you are bright enough to write one. How do I know? From personal experience, that's how.

A friend looked fantastic. She was happy, glowing, had lost weight, and told me she had been awarded Slimmer of the Week at her local slimming club. When I asked about her diet she confessed to not being on one. She had been having an affair. 'We use up a lot of calories,' she said.

I wanted to write this as a story but it really wasn't suitable material for the women's magazines. Nor was the losing weight theme enough for a novel until I began asking *what if?* What if, in front of all the slimming club members, my friend had been asked how she lost the weight and, looking around, spotted the wife of her lover? She could hardly point at her and say it was due to spending many energetic hours in bed 'with her husband'. That led me to becoming interested in the wife. What if she wasn't the wife? What if her so called 'husband' had made the story up to prevent the affair from becoming too serious? A lot more *what ifs?* followed. Characters emerged. My main character became the 'wife'. I then had to give her some family, some friends, a job and a house to live in. I began writing, trusting that now I had a cast they would perform and lead me to the end. And they did. Even though the novel didn't sell I had a whole new set of personal experiences. I knew the pitfalls, where I had gone wrong and what I would do differently next time.

SLOWING DOWN

Unlike short stories where you have to constantly seek out new plots and new characters, a novel allows you to return to the same cast and the same places each day. Some short story writers make the mistake of trying to cover years or even generations in a story. Their efforts read like outlines for books. But for most, the theme of their story won't be enough for a book. A story has only one main character who is explored. A book needs several and they are explored in far more depth than any story heroine. The pace has to change too. A story covers a short space of time so every word has to count. There is no space for long descriptions, no slower scenes. It can take a while to adjust to this new slower pace. My novel was racing along at short story pace and I needed to learn to slow down. 'Add the frocks and food,' a novelist advised.

The most I would have said about food in a story would be: *Emma cut into the chicken breast . . .* and then dialogue would follow. In my novel I could indulge myself with: *He'd reached the vegetarian options and was relishing the descriptions – creamed parsnip, leek and carrot in a herby sauce, served in a case of chef's cheese pastry – when . . .*

It was the same with clothes. *Jenny put on her tight-fitting red top* in a story, but in the novel – *Pearl was in her Dr Zhivago outfit.*

Long boots, long coat with big fur collar and matching Russian-style hat. She flounced in and sat down. From the confines of her fur muff she produced...

That outfit was once mine, apart from the muff. The secret of slowing my pace wasn't as easy as adding frocks and food, but that certainly helped because it showed me how to enjoy going into details that I would normally have to leave out.

HOW DO I BEGIN?

Only you can answer that. You have to find your own way. Some writers swear by outlines or plans. They outline the whole story in careful, methodical detail. They plan each scene, make studies of each character and know exactly where they are heading each day. Others do it the scary way and wing it, not knowing where their book is going to lead them, what is going to happen to each character or even who their characters are. Another way, somewhere between these, is to make lots of notes including scenes and bits of dialogue and description as you think of them so that when the thinking is over, and you have an idea of where your book is going to lead you, there will also be several thousand words already written in one form or another. This method means you never begin with a blank page or screen.

By the time you finish your novel, or even if you never do, you will have another experience to add to your file. And writing a novel is an experience. A writer can discover all sorts about themselves and how their brain works. You might learn that 'my character came alive and insisted on doing this' is not a myth. That is a truly wonderful experience. It may dawn on you that, in the darkest recesses of your brain, your novel is being planned out without you knowing about it because, one day, you write something quite unexpected, decide to turn back the pages to add a few little details so that this unexpected event is not so unforeseen and find that the details leading up to it are already there. Writing a novel is a life enhancing experience.

USING PERSONAL EXPERIENCE

It has been said that first novels are often autobiographical. This does not mean that the main character, or any other character, is you and the story is that of your life. What it means is that a lot of your own personal experiences will go into your work. It makes sense to write about what you know. If a nurse writes a hospital romance then she will know intimately the day to day routine of hospital life. A model will not only know about the catwalk that the public sees, but also what happens behind the scenes, and it would make sense for her to write novels set in this glamorous world she knows so well.

If your world isn't glamorous then it will still be interesting to others. It is not only the setting of novels that attract readers, it is the characters who inhabit them. People are more interested in people than anything else.

Jane Wenham-Jones believes that when you come to write your first novel it is inevitable that a lot of your own life will end up in there. She says:

> *'When I started writing* Raising the Roof *(Bantam) I'd been trying my luck at the buy-to-let market with a builder friend. We'd bought a couple of run-down houses and converted them into flats to rent out. I'd had visions of a property empire*

stretching the length of the Kent Coast and retiring early to count my millions, but it didn't quite work out like that. We had police raids and absconding tenants and tenants who unfortunately didn't abscond but moved all their friends in and then stopped paying the rent. Flats were trashed, doors kicked in, interest mounted and bank managers began to twitch. It was nothing if not a learning curve! But it was also perfect fodder for a novel with plenty of opportunity for comedy – I knew absolutely nothing about building when I started and made all sorts of mistakes – as well as some serious stuff as my heroine spiralled down into debt and despair. It's always good writing about a world you know something about – saves all that tedious research – and as the book came out around the time the buy-to-let market was really starting to take off, it got plenty of interest with many readers saying they found it a refreshing change from the more usual chick-lit scenarios.'

Jane explored the world of building and buy-to-let. How many worlds do you know? You will have some listed in your personal experiences file under jobs, skills, collections, hobbies and interests. If you are, or have been, a child-minder, a bank manager, a carpenter or a bored housewife you will know about these worlds and could use them as settings or plots for your book. If one of your hobbies is bird watching then you will know enough about the world of 'twitchers' to set a novel in it. Where was your childhood spent? Living in a huge house, a small one, a commune, a tent? You could write a novel about the area where you lived or use a house you once lived in as a home for one of your characters.

Christina Jones wrote her third novel *Stealing The Show* because no-one had ever written a novel about fairgrounds from the inside.

'My dad was a fairground traveller,' she says. 'I grew up on fairgrounds; fairgrounds were (and still are) my second home. I've lost track of the number of times I've screamed over fictional fairgrounds where a gang of illiterate and impoverished nomadic ne'er-do-wells drift aimlessly around setting up their horse-drawn caravans and ancient death-trap rides wherever they think they can fleece the gullible public. As an insider, I had to set the record straight – hence Stealing The Show. *Fairs are modern, hi-tech, strictly run, Health and Safety monitored, close-knit, big business hierarchies. Showmen have to belong to and adhere to the rules of the Showmen's Guild; live in trailers or living wagons – never caravans; use their considerable wealth to send their children to expensive private schools; have a "caste system" for marriage and a scarily high moral code; the sites are centuries old and charter-given; and woe betide anyone who steps outside these guidelines. Showmen are a breed apart – they're not gypsies, Romanies, new-agers or tinkers. For me, writing* Stealing The Show *because I* knew *the fairground world inside out was a labour of love and I enjoyed every minute of it.'*

Christina's advice is: 'Write about what you know – a phrase hurled at every embryo writer is one which, in my opinion, should be engraved on the heart of all who put finger to keyboard. There is nothing to beat personal experience: look, if you've never done *it,* touched *it,* smelled *it,* tasted *it,* heard *it – how on earth can you describe it accurately and convincingly to anyone else? So do yourself a favour and use your personal experiences in your novel and your story will simply sing from the page.'*

EXERCISE

List some of the big problems life has thrown at you – the tragedies, shocks, traumas and challenges you have struggled to overcome.

Any one, or two, or all of these could become the basis of your novel. Adversity, pain and sadness can inspire because it is strength, persistence and love that helps us overcome them. Added together, the bad and good, the lows and highs are the forces which carry a novel to its conclusion.

Pam Fudge had a positive approach to the loss of love:

> '*I was totally unprepared for my husband Eddie's sudden death at the age of 52 and thought the odds of finding love again were remote, but I was wrong and remarried three years later. With my second husband Frank's support, my enthusiasm for fiction writing returned, but after only four years I was widowed again, very suddenly, and again I struggled to find the real me – the writer.*
>
> '*It wasn't easy but I felt my choice was to be sad that I had loved and lost – twice – or glad for the love that was mine for a while. The latter worked well for me and when I decided to write a novel its theme was coping with widowhood and getting out into the world again. I didn't have to try very hard to put myself in my heroine, Denise Moffat's shoes in order to write* Widow on the World. *I had always tried to follow the advice,* Write about what you know, *but had no idea that one day I would be taking that advice quite so literally.*'

Avoiding using personal experience as therapy

Don't be tempted to use your experiences as therapy and pour out all your woes onto the paper. Pam Fudge's main character was a strong feisty woman, rather like Pam herself, who saw the positive side of her predicament and set about making a new life for herself. Readers do not want to spend their time with a heroine who is weeping and wailing on every other page. If your traumas are still too close, now may not be the time to tackle them in fiction. Leave them until you can look back without it all feeling too raw and, even then, if you begin to write and feel as if you are picking at the scab on your wound, postpone it once more.

On the other hand, *not* putting distance between yourself and your main character who is going to undergo your trauma may make your writing stronger if you write it when all the events are fresh. Only you can decide which way will suit you.

Including dedications

Widow on the World is dedicated to the memory of Pam's two husbands. She says that knowing it would be dedicated to her two special men helped her to complete it. Beginning with the dedication helped me write my children's novel. *In memory of Duncan*, were the first words I wrote. Duncan, a close family friend, had been killed when cycling to work. We all missed him but it was ten years after his death that I was able to write about him and use him exactly as remembered as one of my main characters. Seeing the dedication every day helped me focus on the work. Try it for yourself.

Fictionalising personal experiences

You've never danced naked on the Town Hall steps? It doesn't matter. You can use your own life story as a basis for your novel and then make it more interesting. Make it more exciting. Marry the man/woman you always thought you should have. Marry several. Be rich, talented, handsome/beautiful. Dance naked. Give the new you – your main character – permission to do all the things you have never had the courage or opportunity to do. Let him or her take your life one step further. Two steps... but remember to call on your personal experiences to guide them through what it feels like to be in love, have a child, lose a job...

Keep asking yourself what if? What if I had taken all my clothes off? What if I had been arrested? What if I had thought I was totally alone as it was the early hours of the morning, but someone was watching?

Think of a point in your life when you had a choice. Shall I say yes? Shall I say no? If you said no then imagine the parallel universe in which you said yes and your life changed direction. Using this method your characters can have all the lives you've ever wanted (or are, at this moment, living in another universe).

Several years ago Eileen Ramsay was at a family wedding in Italy. The ceremony was held in the town square and during the signing of the register a pianist on a balcony began to play. Eileen recalls:

> *'I can still feel the unbelievable hot Italian sun and I can see the faces of the old ladies in black who peered out of all the windows in the houses that surround the square. I hear the pianist too but it is no longer the talented young woman who was there but the internationally famous Raffaele de Nardis for fiction is now mixed with what was reality. Standing there all those years ago, I found myself saying, What if that pianist was... and what if*

the woman standing here in her lemon dress was...and before the wedding was over I had the bones of the story that became A Way of Forgiving *(Hodder & Stoughton). At the beginning of the novel a herd of galloping horses frightens the heroine as she tries to find a villa in the dark; believe me, every quiver of her fear was mine because it did happen and luckily my husband was driving or it's unlikely that the story would ever have been told.*

'Experiences don't have to be exotic. You yourself are your own greatest source. You know what it is like to be frightened, to worry, to fall in love, to hope, to despair, to feel hurt, pain, ecstasy. Mine those experiences and your words will have authenticity.'

CHOOSING THE GENRE

Readers have preferences and will often seek out one type of book. They want crime novels, or historicals, romance or chick-lit. Which genre will your life fit into? How many genres could it fit into? The story of how you fell in love could be turned into chick-lit, straight romance or historical fiction. It depends on how you use it. It is possible to take your account of falling in love, and the opposition you encountered, back in time. Instead of it all happening in the late 20th century or the early 21st, it could be set in Victorian England or any other time which appeals. It is also possible to bring your grandparents' story into the present day. Time is not an obstacle in fiction.

Turning family stories into a saga

Is your family worthy of a novel? A saga? Mine is! My grandmother told me of a relative who had died of a broken heart, another who received anonymous letters in which the sender threatened to steal her child. Then there is the story of the Adam's millions in which we were supposed to be millionaires but the Adam did not leave a will and we, as a family, could not prove we were the closest relatives and had never had enough money to employ a solicitor to prove it for us. This story has been in the family for generations.

While exploring the Hackles' family tree we discovered that grandfather had two brothers. He had never mentioned them. A little research enabled us to discover that one great-uncle died in Baghdad during WWI. The other, according to an aunt who had kept notes and records, ran away to join the army when he was 14 and was never heard of again. What happened to him? There is no death certificate so what if he died abroad and no one knew his name? What if he didn't die? Why were these two young men never spoken of? Have we discovered the skeletons in the family cupboard? Would some of the facts, the personal knowledge I have of the family, mixed together with a huge helping of fiction make a novel? Of course it would.

Could you write a family saga using your own relatives? Could your family tree provide you with enough inspiration for a novel? Could you write a series of novels based on the same character, or different generations? Are there any family mysteries for you to resolve? You can use fiction to fill in the gaps. If there are skeletons in your cupboard, open it up, rattle those bones and write about your family's personal experiences.

Kate Furnivall's book, *The Russian Concubine,* (LittleBrown), is set in China, in 1928. Kate says:

'It was inspired by my mother's childhood as a fleeing White Russian after the Communist revolution in 1917. She, and her mother, escaped eastward to China and it was the stories of her life there that seduced me into exploring that extraordinary time and country. I adored writing it and enjoyed the connection to my roots. There is something about the creative process of using personal experiences that gives an intimacy to the words that is hard to replicate with just cold research – however diligently performed. Though I did of course research the necessary facts about Russia and China, my emotional understanding of those facts came from my personal involvement in my own family's past story. This, for me, gave the book its beating heart.'

Writing crime

The crime you write about needs to be big enough to make a book. Petty pilfering is not going to be enough to keep the reader glued to several hundred pages. Your reader needs to care that this crime is solved and the perpetrator caught and punished. A robbery would have to be a good one, like the Great Train Robbery. Years ago I spent an evening planning a bank robbery. It was during a recession when very little money was coming in and I had read in the local paper that 'our' two policemen were expected to cover a huge area. All I had to do was arrange for them to be called out to the farthest corner they patrolled and then, with chosen accomplices, we could break into the bank. As we were responsible citizens with no criminal records it should have been possible to get away with it. Would it be? My life of crime didn't get further than thinking about it but the beginning of a plot is there.

Personal experience can be used for writing murders too. This doesn't mean that you have to commit murder in order to write about it. We may all have felt like committing murder at some time but we don't take those extra steps. So who does, and why? Those are the questions. The answers will give you murderer and motive. How many murders have we all heard about from television reports and newspaper features? Most of us speculate as to what might have happened and to who might have committed the crime. Take that speculation onto the page and write it.

> *'Personal experience is often the starting point to my novels,' says crime writer, Lesley Horton, 'particularly experiences gleaned during my work in an educational unit for pregnant schoolgirls. For instance* Devils in the Mirror *was conceived when I met a young pregnant girl of mixed race. Her father was from Pakistan and her mother Afro-Caribbean. She had been brought up in the Muslim faith, but when the marriage ended her mother insisted she turn her back on her former way of life and specifically on her religion. At 14 she found it too difficult and saw herself as an infidel and a sinner. Her punishment was to see devils taunting her each time she looked in the mirror.*

> *'The idea reached maturity when some years later a colleague of mine was falsely accused of assaulting a boy in his class, and was finally born when I came across a card advertising a self-styled psychoanalyst's skill at performing black magic and his ability to cast out the evil spirits locked in the souls of the weak.*

> *'What if, I thought, a troubled girl accuses a teacher of assaulting her but changes her story at the last minute? What if that teacher, believing he has been exonerated receives a letter telling him that although innocent in law, the governors need to*

hold their own enquiry? And what if the girl is then found dead in a place where modern paganism is alive? I had my title and my plot line.'

If modern policing and forensics put you off because you have no personal experience of them create a detective who doesn't belong to the police. Take a look in your list of ten interesting people you know. Mix a couple up and come up with an unlikely sleuth. Or set your murder in a bygone era, well before DNA, fingerprints and all the complicated methods in current use.

David Wishart uses his personal experience to write about his amateur detective, Marcus Corvinus who lives in Rome in the 1st Century AD. 'The largest contributing factor,' says David, 'is the general one: my degree is in Classics, so I'm fairly comfortable with the broad background to my books and reasonably certain – touch wood! – that I won't drop any major factual clangers. It's easy for a writer who doesn't have a grounding in the period he's writing in to over-compensate; to bring in a whole lot of background material (specially mugged up for the purpose) which is extraneous to the needs of the plot, just to satisfy – they think – the reader with their credentials. I always like to work on the iceberg principle: one tenth of the research (the relevant stuff) in the book, the other nine-tenths in the writer's mind to give the one-tenth stability. What I do is use, where possible, an actual historical event (or object) as a hook to hang a completely fictitious story onto.'

Personal experience in the form of Annie, David's dog, found abandoned in France several years ago, has also been included in his work. According to David, 'Annie is a character, in both senses of the word. I used her undiluted, flatulence and all, in In at the Death.'

Writing romance

Romance covers all categories. Take one couple and make their romance comical, sensual, dangerous. Bring in a crime. Make the setting an historical one. Make it contemporary. There are many, many variations on the romance so if you want to write about your own romantic encounter it can easily be disguised by adding other elements.

Use your first kiss, remember the way you felt on your first date. Use your emotions and give them to your hero or heroine. And, when it comes to sex, stick with what you are comfortable with. Some writers get as far as the bedroom door while others happily slide beneath the sheets.

EXERCISE

Take five minutes. Lock yourself away from all interruptions and write a sex scene. No-one is looking over your shoulder, no-one is ever going to read this unless you want them to.

Is it any good? Did you enjoy writing it? If your page is blank, or all scribbled out, then you probably shouldn't bother with the more explicit material. But if you are happy with what you've written, or you wrote for ten or fifteen minutes then erotic writing could be your forte.

Writing erotica

Author and anthologist Mitzi Szereto is the pioneer of the erotic writing workshop in the UK and Europe and has more than a dozen books to her credit. She has also penned several best-selling erotic novels under the name M. S. Valentine and has this advice for erotic writers.

'When it comes to erotic writing or, for that matter, any *form of sexually explicit or sexually oriented writing, there's this assumption that the writer is writing about her/himself. This very assumption is possibly the main reason why so many writers censor themselves. It's this titillation factor that presupposes that every writer of sexually oriented prose must be writing about her/himself. Yet such assumptions are rarely, if ever, made about say a Stephen King or Val McDermid. All of us draw upon memory, personal experience, the experiences of friends or family, what we read or see in the news. And yes, there are some erotic writers who write mostly from reality. Personally, the vast majority of my work has been fictional, although I will admit that recently I've been incorporating more elements from my own life both in storylines and sexual scenarios.'*

Writing fantasy

How can personal experience be any part of fantasy writing? Fantasies are set in imaginary worlds, magic is often involved and heroes set off on quests or in search of great adventures. Fantasies are imaginative writing. This is true but these strange worlds are populated by human-like characters and the heroes have our sense of justice. They know what is good and what is evil and their destinies are to fight the forces of evil.

Whoever your fantasy hero is he will have human traits and these can come from your own life experiences. If you have ever been angry because of an injustice, if you have ever wanted to right a wrong, fight for what you believe in or make a difference to your world then you will know how your hero feels. Use your emotions to trigger his actions.

RECAP

Write about:

+ What you know – see your Personal Experiences file.
+ Who you know – use friends as characters or write about their lives.
+ Where you know – places you have lived in and loved, or loathed.
+ What you feel – use emotions you have experienced yourself.

10

Writing for Children

Writers tend to remember their childhoods in vivid detail. They can recall what happened when they were five, seven, fourteen... If you are one of these kinds of writers and can recollect how it felt to be a child then you should consider writing for children. You need to be able to get into the skin of the child you are writing about.

EXERCISE

Get out your Personal Experiences file, go back to the first ten years of your life and describe the following:

◆ A particular outfit you wore on a certain day.

◆ A visit to a doctor/dentist.

◆ Visiting an ancient relative.

◆ An argument with a best friend.

◆ That time you wished you'd never been born.

Growing up is a time of learning. Yes, there is school but children have to learn about life too and how to cope with what life throws at them. These problems can often be the starting point for children's novels.

As children we had limited knowledge of the world around us. There were things that we did not understand. On occasions we were scared but wouldn't always admit it. Now we are grown-up we have hopefully learned a lot and can look back and laugh at some of those fears. When we write, as adults, for children, we can give our grown-up wisdom to our young heroes and heroines. We can guide them in the right direction so that their problems can be solved.

WHY DO YOU WANT TO WRITE FOR CHILDREN?

You could have a go at Mills and Boon, turn to crime, write a best-seller or a non-fiction book? Cookery maybe. You could write for magazines, write poetry, crime or erotica and stand more chance with any of those markets. Why do you want to write for children?

- ◆ It's an easy way into the world of writing.
- ◆ You want to make money.
- ◆ You want to write for your children/grandchildren.
- ◆ It's the only thing you've ever wanted to do.

It's easy

If you think writing for children is easier because the books are shorter and the language simple, then think again. The children's market is the hardest of all to break into and...

Money

...when you do, you don't get rich. (Let's leave J. K. Rowling out of this. Her story, so far, is a one-off.) You rarely get rich. I made peanuts out of my children's book. I have been paid more for a short story. When I went to hear a successful children's author give a talk I cornered him afterwards and asked for his opinion. Was I being ripped off? The answer was no. The sum I received was the same advance as he was getting.

For the children

You have written stories for your children/grandchildren and they love them. This is because you are their parent/grandparent and they would love anything you read to them. Children are not very good critics when it comes to loved ones. They are far more critical when a book has been written by a stranger and will give up on one quite quickly unless the subject matter holds their attention and the writer has drawn them immediately into the story.

All you ever wanted

If writing for children is all you have ever wanted to do then get on with it. You won't be thinking of money, or appreciative little relatives. You won't care whether it is an easy market to break into, or not. You just want to do it. You want the thrill of holding in your hands a book that you have written.

You could make it with any of the above motives but the most likely one to help you succeed is the last. You have to want to write for children, and you need to enjoy it.

The good news is that sales of children's books are on the up. This is a flourishing market.

BEFORE YOU START

Decide what sort of book you want to write, then look in the shops and libraries to see who publishes that type of book. Ask yourself who is going to read your book – what age group? Boys? Girls? Both?

It might happen the other way around. You see a book in the library and think you could write one like that. A subject springs to mind ... If it is a series you have decided to write for it is worth checking that the publishers are still using that series, and will be by the time you have completed your book. If a company is taken over, and this happens all the time now, your chosen series could be scrapped. But others will take its place.

My experience of getting published

My experience of getting a book published has been described as the perfect way. I did exactly what the how to books tell you. I read hundreds of children's books because my ambition was to write them. Then, one day, whilst browsing in the children's library I found a series about sport. I borrowed half a dozen books in the series. They were all fictional stories involving a sport. I checked the number of words, the age group aimed at, the way the books had been written, which was to combine a fast-paced exciting story with real facts about the sport being covered. The books listed included football, cricket, swimming ... there was nothing about cycling and this is where personal experience came in. I knew all about cycle racing. My husband and son were involved in it. After a race half the local cycling club turned up in my kitchen waiting to be fed. I had listened to them talk about their experiences. I had studied training manuals. I had a racing bike of my own and had once – and that was enough for me – competed in a ten mile time-trial.

I wrote to the publishers explaining how there was a gap in their particular market – racing cycling – and telling them I was the right person to fill it. They phoned to say they were interested but warned that if another writer offered the same subject they would look at that too. No promises then. But it was enough for me.

I wrote *Racing Start* (Blackie & Son) in six weeks. Most of it was based on the personal experiences of me, my family – especially my son – and our best friend, Duncan. My personal experience of a ten mile time-trial was included when my young hero tackled his first time-trial. I knew exactly how he would feel – the breathlessness, the pain, the lungs bursting and pulses thumping.

WRITING FOR DIFFERENT AGE GROUPS

You too can draw on your personal experiences when writing for children. You can also use your own children's experiences, your grandchildren's, the kids' next door. Everyone has had a childhood and each one has been unique. You may feel drawn to one particular age group more than any other. If you love babies and toddlers then picture books may be the way to go. If your fondest memories are of your early schooldays then you may have ideas for easy-readers or exciting stories for children who have reached the stage where they are capable of tackling a book on their own. If your teen years were dramatic, traumatic or the best time of your life then this age group could be your target audience. You do not need to know children of that age in order to write for them. Why? Because you've been there yourself, you've experienced that age so you are fully qualified to write for it.

By the end of this chapter there will be something in your Personal Experiences file which will supply you with an idea, or two, or more. In all probability you will have something to suit each age group.

Writing picture books

Let's begin with picture books. These range from the first books children have. Often made from cloth or thick card these deal with the experiences very young children are familiar with. The main problem new writers have with picture books is that they (a) do not realise how difficult the market is, and (b) do not understand how to set them out.

Picture books are nice and short, take very little time to write and must therefore be easy. No! The picture book market is actually the hardest of all to break into.

Considering the layout

Borrow or buy a picture book. Open it and count the pages. You will find they come in multiples of four. A 32 page book could have a dozen words in it or a thousand. Count how many pages contain the story. You can discount several as they will be for the title and publisher's information. The story probably begins on page 5 and covers 25 pages of the 32 available. This means that you have to cut your story up into 25 sections because it will need to fit on those 25 pages. Some pages could be pictures only, most will have some text too. And the good news is that you do not have to supply the pictures. By studying picture books you will see that many have an author and an artist listed.

EXERCISE

You have already written down your earliest memory. Continue from there until the age of five when you started school. These memories could include some, or all, of the following:

◆ Siblings being born.
◆ Moving house.
◆ Getting lost.
◆ Losing a pet or toy.

◆ Being sick.

◆ Going into hospital.

◆ Having spectacles.

◆ Going to nursery.

At least one or two of the above will be amongst your personal experiences or your children's and/or grandchildren's. It is how we all use them that matters. You may have adored your baby sister when she arrived, or you may have been jealous. Moving house could have been exciting or terrifying. When I was five our family moved into the next street and I began having a recurring dream in which I would walk home from school and discover that my house wasn't where it was supposed to be.

Did you have to stay in hospital when you were tiny? Was it a scary experience? A good way for children to read about scary things is to change the main character into an animal or toy. Children feel safer reading about a sick bear who has to have an operation, rather than another child. Picture books often contain learning experiences. Have you ever found yourself explaining to a child why they should not be scared of the dentist? Shadows in the dark? A boisterous dog? Mummy going away for a few days? Is there anything on your list which would make a picture book?

2–3,000, 5000, 10,000...

Different age groups have different length books. 50,000 words would be too daunting for a child who has just learned to read. Make sure you know which age group you are writing for and stick to a suitable length, language and subject. You need to do your market research. Haunt the libraries and bookshops. Read what today's children are reading. If your book is meant for 10–12 year olds then make your main character almost 13 because children don't read about characters younger than themselves. Do not have a 12 year old carrying a doll around with her unless it's the whole point of the story – she's taking it to her little sister at crèche, it falls out of her bag and her friends see it and tease her.

Writing for children is a huge responsibility. If a child read your book and didn't like it he/she could be put off books for life. Think about your love of books. You want to give this same joy of reading to a new generation. What if you were to write a science fiction story for 6–8 year olds? It might be the first sci-fi a child of that age had come across in book form, and if he/she didn't like it they might never read another, and then they'd miss out on *The War of the Worlds*, *The Day of the Triffids*, all the great classics and all of the great new authors of sci-fi.

Think back to the first books you enjoyed. Who were your favourite authors? Weren't these the people who influenced you, who gave you your love of reading, and writing?

Now forget them because most – not all, there are classics – are old fashioned and out of date. You would get nowhere duplicating them. What you need to remember is the way they made you feel when you read them, and duplicate that feeling. There was the wonder of getting lost in a story, the escapism. The magic and adventure that carried us from the page and into that fictional world. Did you want to escape for a while from your own life and share a more exciting one where grown-ups did not interfere in children's secret lives? There were characters we wanted to be like, or even change places with. There was a sense of belonging.

Hands up those who *didn't* want to be in the Famous Five, sail to Treasure Island or find a door in the back of the wardrobe?

What did you want out of a story? A happy ending, hope for a brighter future for the characters we were reading about? Justice? Entertainment? Escapism? Adventure?

Nothing has changed. Children want exactly the same as we did. They too want to share the excitement, the fear, the despair, sorrow and joy of the characters in the books they read. This is why, even if you do not have children or grandchildren of your own, if you don't have contact with children in your work or social life, or even if you do not know a single child, you can still write for this market. All you have to do is write for the child you used to be, and that child may not be too far away. Time is a strange concept and events from years ago can seem as clear as if they happened yesterday. We age on the outside but don't have to on the inside where the child we once were, still is.

EXERCISE

Travel back now to your first day at school. Was it magical or miserable? What memories do you have from those early schooldays?

◆ Falling out with friends.
◆ Accidents.
◆ Friends moving away or dying.
◆ Disliking, or loving, a teacher.
◆ Pets.
◆ Did you have a secret hiding place? Was it small for little treasures, or large enough for you to hide in?
◆ Do you remember learning to read? I not only swapped books with the

boy sitting next to me, we also swapped spectacles. The books we
used were numbered and I couldn't wait to reach Book 12, the last in
the series, and begin on something else.

Writing easy-reads

The books children learn to read from are short and simple.
Later, when they can read alone the books are between 2,000 and
3,000 words and split into short chapters. The young reader gets a
sense of achievement because they have read a *whole* chapter.
Each chapter will end at an exciting point so that the child will
want to carry on reading to find out what happens next. A writer
has to hold the child's interest from start to finish. Subjects are
varied and are often set in the environments children of that age
are familiar with – home and school. Many of these books are
also humorous. One of my favourites was about a vampire who
had toothache. The dentist took his fangs out. He had to become
a werewolf after that.

Do you have anything on your list you can use, or embroider on?
A personal experience from that age that can be turned into a
story?

Writing for 8–12 year olds

Your reader is now older and has more experience. The subject
range can cover almost anything. Children between the ages of 8
and 12 often have better social lives than their parents. There are
sports and hobbies, after-school activities and parties. The
possibilities are there for more adventure because this age group
is not always supervised. There is more interaction with friends.
There are more secrets from parents. There is more awareness of

what is going on around them. At five, a child may not realise that their parents are falling out or a relative is sick. An older child is more likely to know that something is wrong. There is also a growing awareness of self and a need to 'fit in' with others.

EXERCISE

Transport yourself back to those years between the ages of 8 and 12. What happened to you during that time?

◆ What was happening in your family life?

◆ What was going on at school?

◆ You would have changed schools during this time. How did that feel?

◆ Did you belong to any clubs?

◆ Who was your best friend?

◆ Who did you dislike? And why?

◆ Was there one thing that set you apart from others?

Consider the problems that faced you as you were growing up. Look at your list and ask a few *What ifs?*. Here are a few examples from my own list:

◆ What if when I fell through the window, I'd lost my leg instead of slicing it in half?

◆ What if the faulty electric fire I switched on had burned the house down?

◆ What if my little brother had been killed by that car (instead of nudged) when I was supposed to be looking after him?

◆ What if when I ran away from home, I'd got farther than the end of the street? What if I'd ended up lost or slipped through time?

What if any of the above had really happened? What sort of stories would they make? Horror? Science fiction? Time-slip?

Time-slip stories are popular. Imagine how one of today's children would cope slipping back in time to . . . when? Days without computers, central heating, cars, electricity. What have you lived through that today's children would have no experience of? Make a quick list NOW.

Depending on the amount of personal experience you have, other experiences could be added to the list. You may have experience of living through the war, the abdication of the king, a couple of Coronations – events of national and international importance. These childhood experiences – wartime, '50s, '60s, any decade – could be used in a time-slip or historical story, and today's children will enjoy reading about them. Because you lived then you can make your story authentic by using your personal experiences.

Drawing on problems

What sort of problems have you lived through? There are the external ones, like wars, floods, fires, natural disasters. These were all beyond your power to change. There were probably traumas closer to home, in your family life – parents splitting up, sickness, death, accidents . . . Did you try to change the course of these events? You may have tried to keep your parents together by pleading with them, threatening them with what you would do if one left . . . You may have made a pact with God – 'If you do this for me then I will do that for you.' What if you could have changed events in this way? There lies the story.

EXERCISE

List the big problems from as far back as you can remember, right up until you left school. These could include any of the above, or bullying, fighting, suicide, depression, discovering a secret and being unable to tell anyone . . . Take one of those major problems and use the what if? principle or the parallel universe technique, and see if either method leads you to a story.

On a brighter note

Humour is popular. A funny story can still contain a big problem, even a life or death one, but can be treated in a more light-hearted way. A main character might be clumsy or feel useless but still work through the problem you give them in their own unique way. For example my dog nearly starved himself to death once because I had broken the only dish he had ever eaten from. No other dish would do, and I tried all sorts. The broken dish had been a disgusting dark brown and was a thick cheap pottery monstrosity. Eventually, before Fons wasted away altogether, I found a pub ashtray that he approved of. It advertised tobacco around the outside of it and I was trying to work out ways of scratching this off when it was pointed out to me that dogs can't read.

I transferred what had happened to me, as an adult, into a child's life. Fons's owner, and the breaker of the precious dish, became a 12-year-old boy. The age and sex didn't matter because the feelings of guilt at breaking the dish, concern over the dog's deteriorating health and the problem of finding something he would eat from were all exactly the same as I had experienced. (The story *Dog's Dinner*, appeared in a collection, *Don't Make Me Laugh*, published by William Heinemann.)

Has anything happened in your adult life that you could transfer
to a child's?

Writing for young adults

Some would-be writers are frightened of writing for today's teens.
'But children today are so different to how we were,' they say.
Wrong! The world may have changed. Technology has arrived in a
big way but it is so fast-moving and ever-changing that writers are
recommended not to include too much of it in their writing as it
would be out-dated before their book gets into print.

The world, our environments, have changed but childhood
problems remain the same – peer pressure, bullying, concerns
about school, worrying about spots or being unattractive, feeling
that you don't fit in, wanting a girlfriend or boyfriend. Today's
teenagers are not an alien species. They have the same problems
as we did at their age.

What happened in your teens that you could write about? What
has happened to your own teenagers that you could use? Or
happened to someone else's you have contact with? Here are a few
ideas – jobs, school, exams, appearance, relationship with parents,
grandparents, siblings, friends and members of the opposite sex.
Or if you fancy tackling something stronger – drugs, anorexia,
teenage sex, pregnancy, homelessness, shoplifting, vandalism.

EMOTIONS

This was the time of your life when you were forming your own
opinions, questioning what was going on around you and
disobeying all those stupid rules. Life and its problems were all so
dramatic back then. A spot on the end of your nose was the end

of the world. A friend betraying you could turn you into a recluse for a week. You struggled with overwhelming feelings of injustice. There were times when you wanted to end it all because you couldn't see a future. No-one loved you or was ever going to. And it was definite that no-one understood you. Parents forced you into doing 'stuff' you didn't want to do. Teachers put on the pressure over exams, good results, good behaviour... If any of that brought back memories then the teen market could be the way for you to go.

Real life situation books are very popular. Books that deal with tough subjects such as death and divorce, step-parents, bullying, homelessness, living in a B&B, teen pregnancy, abortion and even incest. This type of book does a job. It lets young people, who may be going through the same situation, know that they are not alone. It also allows them to see that their problem can be dealt with. It may even give them ideas of how to overcome it. And if a reader has led a quiet and protected life this type of book allows them out of their comfort zone. They can safely explore the grief, fear and passion of their contemporaries even though they have never experienced the same situations.

If you have experience of any dramatic situation then you will have material for the real life fiction market for young adults. However, every diet should be varied, and reading material is no exception so shelves are filled with other genres too.

Genres

Whether you opt for historical, crime, science-fiction or fantasy you can still use your personal experiences. Your hero wields a magical sword and can transport himself across miles with a special click of his fingers. You won't have personal experience of either but you do know what is right and what is wrong and having a sense of justice would be a big part of your hero. He falls in love. You know what that feels like. He is hurt, physically or emotionally – you will have experienced this at some stage of your life. You transfer your outlook on life, your emotions and personal experiences to your hero.

SETTINGS

Have you, as an adult, ever revisited a place you loved when you were young? Had it changed? Was it smaller than you remembered? Duller? Had the magic been lost? It's happened to most of us but, in our memories, the original exciting place still lives on and we can use that one to write about.

As discussed before, settings can be the place from where your story springs. You enter a cave, an old building, a village and you know that this is where you want to place a story. You remember a house you loved, a school you hated, a shop you regularly visited. Perhaps they do not physically exist any longer but they are still in your mind and you have the power to rebuild them!

On a smaller scale writers can use their personal experience of places and add them to a story. I have replicated my attic bedroom from my teenage years in a story for young adults. Same room, same colour scheme. I moved my furniture into my heroine's room and allowed her to stand on the same old oak chest as I did in order to look out of the window. Her wardrobe was in the same place as mine and she even had the same hiding place as I did – a loose board beneath a rug. Then I gave her two items that would never have crossed my mind when I was that age

– only because these particular luxuries weren't even dreamed of in those days. My heroine had a television set and a small en-suite shower room in one corner. The latter was only because her step-father was a plumber.

If you can see the places you are writing about then your reader will be able to see them too.

CHARACTERS

Think back, once again, to the children's books you enjoyed. Remember the characters in them and consider which ones you wanted to be like when you were growing up. What is it about those particular characters that makes them remain in your memory years after you read about them?

And what about the baddies? Do you remember them? How many times have you looked at someone and instantly made up your mind as to whether you are going to like them or not? If you were to write a description of someone this applied to would your reader also dislike them?

EXERCISE

List six childhood friends, three girls and three boys. Write a paragraph describing each and explaining why you chose them as friends.

List two unlikeable children from your childhood acquaintances. Write a paragraph describing each and explaining why you didn't like them.

Now do the same with adults – six you liked, a couple you didn't.

In some children's fiction there are characters who are totally good or totally evil. The writer can get away with this depending on what type of story they are writing but if you were using real life and life-like characters would you have a rotten through and through baddie?

In the following, Dan, our hero meets the baddie for the first time. But is Munster Briggs really evil? Is anyone ever 100% bad? Or 100% good?

> Dan looked up at the man on the stage. He was dressed from head to toe in black. His long, above-the-knee leather boots, his long coat, long scarf, even his long hair were jet black. He was a long thin man. The stubble on his chin was black. His skin was pale. He could have played the part of Count Dracula, if it hadn't been for the glint of mischief in his blue-grey eyes and even they were beneath bushy black brows. Suddenly he noticed Dan and smiled. His teeth looked all the whiter against the blackness of him.
>
> So this was the dreaded Munster Briggs, thought Dan. The man didn't look evil. He looked more... full of mischief.

Munster came from personal experience when, at a workshop, I was given a picture of Alice Cooper, the controversial rocker.

From your description of a character would you expect the reader to decide immediately what type of person that was? A goodie or a baddie? Do they need to be able to do that? Could you be stereotyping your character?

Characters in children's books alter with age and range from a simple teddy bear to a complex teenager, or adult. Think carefully about what you knew and understood when you were five, seven, ten, fourteen, whatever the age of your characters.

Who are you?

How did you become the person you are today? Genetics, upbringing, education and environment will all have played a part. They will also play a part in who your characters are and why they behave as they do.

Try writing a character study of yourself then ask yourself why you are who you are.

Now do the same with a fictional character.

WRITING DIALOGUE

How much should you use? That's down to market research again but most children's books have more dialogue than description. If you can make some of it funny, make the style fit the character, give each character a different voice, then you are more than halfway there. Do you speak in the same way to everyone you know? If you were telling a friend about a problem you might swear. If you were telling the vicar about the same thing you almost certainly would not.

Try this. Go back into childhood. Think back to a birthday or Christmas, any time you were given an unwanted gift. For example, let's say that your grandmother has given you a gaudily coloured, hand-knitted sweater.

◆ What would you say to her?

◆ What would you tell your best friend about it?

◆ What would you write about it in your secret diary?

Each situation would differ but you would be the same person. In each case you would be expressing yourself differently. The way a person speaks shows a lot about their character.

◆ Did you tell Gran a white lie?

◆ Did you blurt out what you really felt about the sweater?

◆ Did you deliberately say something cruel in order to hurt her?

Each answer would give your character a different personality. The first would give you a thoughtful, kind child. The second a thoughtless one. The third certainly has problems. Why would they want to be so spiteful?

Did you make a big joke about it with your best friend? Complain bitterly about how mean Gran was? Did you explain to your friend that you were wearing the dreadful sweater in order to make your Gran happy?

What would you write in your diary? Were you wise enough at that age to realise that your grandmother had put a lot of time, effort and love into her knitting? Did you wonder why she hadn't simply given you the money instead? Did you wonder how she could be so stupid as to think you would like, or wear, her gift?

Swearing isn't a good idea in children's fiction but you can make up your own swearwords if you want to or you can suggest, by the reactions of other characters, that your character has been swearing:

Chrissie bowed her head and mumbled into the gaping neck of the hideous sweater. 'Don't swear in front of me,' shouted her father. Or he could have said, '*My Dad would have washed my mouth out if I'd said that.*'

Children speak the same language as we do. They may litter their conversations with the latest words but when writing dialogue do not worry about what the current slang is. Forget about it. Because it dates so quickly it is best not to use it. It is more the content of the conversation, rather than the actual words, which shows how old a child is. It is unlikely they will be discussing politics or tax returns. They are more likely to be talking about clothes, bands and favourite television programmes. Think back to when you were the same age as your character and remember what subjects were uppermost in your thoughts.

Long descriptions are not often used so allow dialogue to impart information and description. It can be used to describe people or places. You could explain what Mrs Dhaliwal looks like in a line or two of description:

Mrs Dhaliwal was as wide as she was tall. She was wearing a bright pink sari and had a long floaty pink and gold scarf around her neck.

Or you could use dialogue to let the reader know:

'*Take a look at Old Dhaliwal,*' giggled Angie.

'*Ooh, she looks lovely in that bright pink sari and that long floaty pink and gold scarf thing around her neck,' said Gemma.*

'Yeah, like a fat parrot,' Angie sniggered.

That not only gives description, it also gives the reader information about the two girls speaking. 'Giggled' and 'sniggered' have been used in preference to said. These words also give information about the speakers. Some how to books will tell you to avoid words like these and stick to 'said' which is invisible but, once again, know your market. Books for older children often use a different word to said.

PLOTTING

You have your main character. He is a friend from schooldays, or the son of a neighbour, or your own son. He, or she, is firmly fixed in your mind. You can see them, and you feel you know them. Now is the time to give them a problem, then add another. Throw in a few smaller ones for good measure.

I based *Racing Start* on my son and my personal experience of cycle racing and cycling clubs. My character was called Steve. I made him the smallest, skinniest boy in his class at school and hopeless at sport. The book begins with him face down in the mud on the football pitch. Being hopeless at sport is his main problem. He desperately wants to be good at it. I made the problem worse by giving Steve an unsympathetic games teacher. On the first page a bully in the class, who appears to be good at everything, discovers in the changing room that little Steve who is 12 years old is wearing underpants with a tag in them that says 'For 6–7 year olds', add to that the fact that they have dinosaurs on them, add to that Steve's Dad was a professional footballer...

Steve has plenty to cope with but underlying all these problems is another one – a psychological one, something inside which he has to overcome. In this case it is Steve's lack of confidence in himself. So that it was not all doom and gloom I gave Steve a best friend, someone to confide in. He certainly needed a friend.

Once you have decided on your main character you give him or her a selection of problems from your own, or other friends' childhoods, and you allow your main character to work through these under his own efforts. In this way you begin to work through the story, drawing on personal experience whenever possible. Your main character's dog dies – you go back to the time you lost a pet. Your character has an accident – you recall one you had. You will know how it feels and put your feelings into the writing.

Once the problems are solved and your character has been through a learning experience and is therefore a better person, you've done your job. You have finished. Some writers have a tendency to waffle on. Do not be one of them. Make sure your end is a satisfying one. If it's not exactly happy, leave an impression of hope. By the end all problems are solved but, and this is important, they will have been solved by your main character's own efforts.

FAIRY GODMOTHERS

Fairy godmothers are banned. Do not have a character appear and solve your main character's problem for them, as happened in Cinderella. Her fairy godmother turned up and solved her problems so she did go to the ball. Why did Cinders sit by the fire and sulk? Why didn't she pull down the curtains, give them a wash and start snipping and sewing and make her own dress?

Think about it. When you were growing up what made you feel good – finishing a project on your own, or having a parent take over and finish it for you? Which was the more satisfying?

DIFFICULT BITS

The difficult bits will be different things to different writers. You could be struggling to write about a first kiss, or you have been putting off writing a scene where a child dies or is injured. This is where you need personal experience. If your first kiss remains in your memory then write about it and transfer the experience to your character. If you have not experienced a child dying or being injured, then write about the closest you have been to death or injury. Shut yourself away on your own and throw yourself into the emotions. Believe that you are writing this for your own eyes only and that no-one else will ever see it unless you decide you want them to. Pour out those personal experiences.

I had to write a piece about a dog being taken to the vets to be put down. It was something I'd had to do so I could draw on personal experience. In order to write it I used my own dog and changed it to the fictional dog afterwards. For me, the writing of this was tough, painful and emotional. And that's exactly how I wanted it to be for the reader.

Nothing works better than personal experience.

Index